ILLEGALLY YOURS

ILLEGALLY YOURS

a memoir

RAFAEL AGUSTIN

GRAND CENTRAL
PUBLISHING

NEW YORK   BOSTON

Grand Central Publishing
Hachette Book Group
1290 Avenue of the Americas,
New York, NY 10104

grandcentralpublishing.com

twitter.com/grandcentralpub

First edition: July 2022

Grand Central Publishing is a division of Hachette Book Group, Inc. The Grand Central Publishing name and logo is a trademark of Hachette Book Group, Inc.

The publisher is not responsible for websites (or their content) that are not owned by the publisher.

The Hachette Speakers Bureau provides a wide range of authors for speaking events. To find out more, go to www.hachettespeakersbureau.com or call (866) 376-6591.

Library of Congress Cataloging-in-Publication Data

Names: Agustin, Rafael, author.
Title: Illegally yours : a memoir / Rafael Agustin.
Description: First edition. | New York : Grand Central Publishing, 2022.
Identifiers: LCCN 2022004300 | ISBN 9781538705940 (hardcover) | ISBN 9781538705964 (ebook)
Subjects: LCSH: Agustin, Rafael. | Ecuadorian Americans—Biography. | Noncitizens—United States—Biography. | Illegal immigration—United States.
Classification: LCC E184.E28 A48 2022 | DDC 973/.0468866—dc23/eng/20220307
LC record available at https://lccn.loc.gov/2022004300

ISBNs: 9781538705940 (hardcover), 9781538705964 (ebook)

Printed in the United States of America

LSC-C

Printing 1, 2022

To my two Violetas

Contents

CONTENTS

ILLEGALLY YOURS

Prologue

The metal bars slammed frighteningly close to my face. I stared at the immigration official on the other side of the cell, wide-eyed. I could not believe what was happening. The nightmare I'd feared as a child was now becoming a reality. I was being deported. Granted, it was not at all how I'd worried it would come to pass. There were no kids. There were no cages. I was being detained in a Spanish jail inside an airport. I didn't even know they had jails inside airports!

I had just flown cross-country from Los Angeles to New York, and then caught a late-night international flight across the Atlantic to Spain. When I exited the plane and walked up to the customs kiosk, the Spanish officer asked for my immigration papers. He was shocked to see my Ecuadorian passport.

"What is this?" he exclaimed.

I said that was my Ecuadorian passport, but not to worry. I was a resident of the United States of America now, and quickly flashed my brand-new, shiny green card. Frustrated, the Spanish officer said, "That doesn't matter. Ecuadorians, Colombians, and Cubans are not allowed in Spain without a special visa." Wait—*what?*

"Since when?" I demanded to know.

"Since last month," said the stone-faced customs official.

I didn't know it at the time, but Spain had just passed a draconian law trying to cut off immigration from certain South American countries, as well as other economically struggling nations, such as Morocco and Poland. Spain opened their borders when they needed cheap labor, and then closed them just as quickly when the work dried up. It dawned on me then that all immigration policy around the world was used the same way by every country: to control labor. But I was not there to work or give a lecture about immigration policy. This was my first trip to Europe and I wanted to wild out like any young, beautiful, reckless American.

I was rushed over to an immigration officer standing nearby, who then marched me over to a hidden office at the airport. The Spanish were so secretive. A new disheveled immigration official arrived, but he refused to speak to me until a lawyer was present to inform me of my rights. A clumsy Spanish lawyer, juggling his coffee and briefcase in the same hand, showed up half an hour later. At least the Spanish legal system was serious about everyone having legal counsel. The lawyer briefly said hi before launching straight into a rapid-fire, legal language exchange in Spanish—lisp and all! I tried to follow along, but it was very difficult to make out. This was not the type of Spanish I'd grown up accustomed to in Southern California. Nodding his head, my lawyer agreed with something the official said, and then the two Madrileños turned to me.

"Why didn't you get a special visa to come?" asked my newly appointed attorney.

Quick on my feet, I replied, "Why the hell did the airline let me fly without me having one?"

The two men launched into another comedic-sounding, rapid-fire legal language exchange in Spanish and then nodded to each other once more. The immigration official picked up the phone, let out one final machine-gun-sounding Spanish exchange over the landline, and then slammed his phone shut.

"Continental Airlines has just been fined five thousand dollars for letting you fly," the official said matter-of-factly.

"What? No! That's not what I wanted to do," I said, suddenly more concerned about the airline's well-being than my own. My lawyer chimed in and tried to explain once more that I was not allowed to be in Spain without a special visa. Annoyed, I snapped and said, "Fine, just send me back home." By *home*, I clarified, I meant the United States—just in case they wanted to send me back on a cheaper flight to South America.

As brave as I sounded on the outside, I was actually starting to panic on the inside. This was my greatest fear personified. In all my years in the United States as an undocumented immigrant, I dreaded one thing and one thing only: deportation. The official stated, "We have no choice but to send you back to the United States." "Fine," I barked back. I didn't care anymore. The excitement to explore the Spanish countryside rocking my George Clooney Caesar haircut completely left my body. This experience could not get any worse. "Unfortunately," added the official, "the next flight doesn't depart until twenty-four hours from now." It was presently 10:30 a.m. in Madrid.

"Okay," I said, finally giving up. "Are you putting me up in a hotel?"

The immigration official gave me a worried look and then stated, "Well... it's not quite a hotel."

Moments later, I glared at the immigration official from the other side of the cell I was locked inside of. To be honest, I was madder at myself. I had hidden my immigration status from American authorities for so long, yet let my guard down on my first trip to Europe. Not that long ago, this would have been a real problem...

American Ninja

The first time I heard the word "America" was as a small child when my mom, grandma, and I took my mom's youngest brother, my uncle Andres, to the José Joaquín de Olmedo International Airport in Guayaquil, Ecuador. My uncle was going to visit family in the United States. I watched him lovingly hug my mom and grandma good-bye.

"May God protect your path every step of the way," said my grandma in Spanish.

My uncle waved at us as he boarded his plane, and we watched the warm headwind help lift that aircraft off into the bright blue tropical sky. I tugged on my mom's dress and asked, "Where's Uncle Andres going?"

"He's going to America," my mom replied.

I didn't take my eyes off the Boeing 747 until I saw the last bit of its tail disappear into the clouds. As far as I knew at four years of age, heaven was the only place that existed in the sky, so I decided that America must be a place in heaven.

This impression was solidified as I got older and began to watch Hollywood action movies. Arnold Schwarzenegger, Jean-Claude Van Damme, and Sylvester Stallone adorned our South American TV screens twenty-four hours a day. I had no idea that two of those movie stars were immigrants to the United States, and that the other was a child of immigrants. I did not know any of this because I could not understand what they were saying. I didn't speak English at the time. Luckily, you never have to translate kicking ass. Seeing Rambo go on a bloody rampage on behalf of the United States meant that America was a place worth dying for. I never saw an Ecuadorian veteran suffering from post-traumatic stress disorder go on a killing spree to defend the honor of fried plantains! But my absolute favorite American hero was American Ninja. *American Ninja* was a film that starred American heartthrob Michael Dudikoff, who went on to star in other great films such as *American Ninja 2: The Confrontation* and *American Ninja 4: The Annihilation*. *American Ninja* was where it all began for me. I was seven years old when I realized, thanks in part to Michael Dudikoff, that I had to devote the rest of my life to becoming both a ninja and an American.

While Rambo and American Ninja were my favorites, my American role models were not limited to the muscle-bound bravado of action heroes. I was also obsessed with DC Comics, Disney cartoons, and the *Lone Ranger*. In other words, I watched a *lot* of American TV as a kid. Most days I was glued to the Spanish-dubbed version of the 1960s *Batman* TV show. At the time, I had no idea that the Joker was portrayed by

Latino actor Cesar Romero, who refused to shave his signature Latin Lover mustache for the show and applied white makeup over it for the duration of the series. I didn't even know what a Latino was back then. As far as I knew, I was just a white South American boy living a cozy existence in his grandparents' relatively large house. I would ask one of our maids to make me a bowl of fresh fruit as I plopped down in front of the TV wearing my Batman Halloween costume. Watching how the caped crusader and his young ward saved Gotham City, USA, was everything to me. That and ripe mangos.

My mom had to save up to buy me that Batman costume as a birthday gift, and I wore it everywhere—to the park, to my friends' houses, to the dinner table. My mom didn't have much money back then. She was a humanitarian at heart, so instead of following the family tradition of law and politics, she decided to become a doctor. In most places around the world, doctors make a lot of money. Not in Ecuador, where medicine is socialized. The socialization of medicine in Ecuador was not the real culprit for the nation's economic decline. In fact, it was quite nice to know you could go to any hospital and get medical care no matter who you were. The real problem in Ecuador has always been foreign intervention and the national leaders that embrace it. In 1980, the year I was born, the democratically elected socialist president of Ecuador died unexpectedly in a plane crash before he could reorganize the hydrocarbon sector, a strong threat to US interests, or before he could nationalize the country's petroleum—the third largest export from Ecuador; and the third largest petroleum source in Latin America. In 1981, the year of my first birthday, the democratically elected socialist president of Panama also died in a similar unexpected plane crash before he could nationalize the Panama Canal, yet another great threat to US interests. Were these "accidental" plane crashes part of Operation Condor, a United States–backed campaign of political repression and state terror involving intelligence operations and assassination of political opponents? Am I asking too many serious questions for a relatively comedic memoir? Possibly. But, YOLO!

My grandpa, on the other hand, was a very influential judge in Guayaquil. On top of that, he built commercial rental properties in front of his house so that my grandma could have an income once he was gone. From my mom's point of view, it was bad enough that she was a single mother living with her parents; she did not want to ask her dad for more help than she deemed necessary. And getting a free commercial rental property in front of their house was not necessary! My earliest memories are of my grandma and me hanging out by the window waiting for my mom to return home from a long day of medical school classes.

After she graduated from medical school and got a job at Guayaquil's largest children's hospital, we continued to live at my grandparents' house. Everything in Guayaquil was done through *palanca* (i.e., connections and influences), and my mom getting her first job as a doctor was no different. She and my biological father, Ronald, had gotten a divorce when I was still an infant. In an attempt to win her back after cheating on her one too many times, Ronald, who was working with the national anti-narcotics department at the time, stepped up to get my mom her first residency. He also did so to get back in the good graces of my grandfather, who had sent him to prison a few years earlier for not paying child support on time. Ronald was trying hard to achieve a level of notoriety as a young attorney, but then he met my mom and her litigious family. My mom never took Ronald back. The great irony is that my mom ended up meeting my stepdad at the same hospital where Ronald got her a job.

My stepdad was a pediatric surgeon who lived in the shadow of his more successful pediatric surgeon father. Older surgeons would rather speak to my stepdad's father than speak to him, and this put a giant Ecuadorian chip on his shoulder. When my mom showed up for her first day of residency, she was warned to stay clear of the hot-tempered head surgeon. Based on this, she expected him to be a towering, grumpy old man. Instead, she was shocked to meet my stepdad, a younger, shorter, skinnier Latin American version of Stephen Colbert. He seemed to be the complete opposite of my biological father: honest, studious, and very direct. My stepdad had a crush on my always-optimistic mom from the moment he met her. Her presence invariably put a smile on his face. But my stepdad had three children with two different women and had just come out of a messy divorce. He figured he should just focus on his surgeries and avoid all the personal distractions.

My mom worked tirelessly through her residency at the hospital. She made time for my birthday, but then I did not see her again. I spent Christmas alone with my grandma and grandfather, wondering what gifts Santa Claus had brought my mom this year. New Year's Eve crept up really fast. Noticing that he was overworked and maybe even in more need of a break than she was, my mom built up the courage to invite my stepdad to one of my grandparents' legendary New Year's Eve parties in Urdesa. He declined the invitation initially, crushing my mom, who was starting to warm up to her superior. But as my stepdad operated alone that December 31 and noticed that the majority of his colleagues had requested time off to be with their families, he thought—*Why am I doing this to myself?*

My stepdad arrived at my grandparents' house and knocked on the front gate two hours before midnight. My dashing uncle Antonio greeted him at the door. My uncle Antonio was a lawyer, my grandmother's firstborn, and even though he was not my grandfather's biological child, he was the one out of all his siblings who most shared my grandfather's strong character. The way my stepdad jokes about it, he would have never gone to the party if he knew my mom already had a son. It was not love at first sight for him. It was the fear of one more child to support at first sight!

Still in his medical scrubs, my stepdad stood out in a sea of collared shirts and neatly pressed guayaberas. He walked through the large family gathering until he reached my grandfather. Of course he knew who Agustín Arrata was; everyone in town did. My grandfather did not know my stepdad, but he did like that a medical professional had come looking for his daughter, so he welcomed the young surgeon into his home.

My stepdad respectfully greeted my grandfather and then proceeded to wait ten excruciating minutes for my mom to come down the stairs, but when she did, she was a sight to behold. She looked different in her nice-fitting blue cocktail dress and with her hair glamorously done. Even her makeup was striking. My mom grew up with a bunch of sisters and inherited all their best tips for properly doing the perfect smoky eyes. My mom and my stepdad awkwardly flirted for about an hour. Everything was going great until I came crying down the stairs. I was tired and wanted the party to be over already. Why wasn't it midnight so everybody could go home? My mom took the opportunity to introduce my stepdad and me. From the second we met, my stepdad treated me like an adult. I was six years old. He firmly shook my hand, while my mom stepped away to check on my grandma and how New Year's Eve dinner, which we usually had around midnight, was coming along. My stepdad and I looked at each other, quietly taking each other in.

I took a quick liking to my stepdad. All the Ecuadorian men in my life up to that point were deceivingly charming. One of my mom's ex-boyfriends played with me only to convince me to tell my mom how much I liked him. The dude wanted me to be his wingman on my own mother! My stepdad was not like that. Or at least, he did not seem to be. He was stern. What you saw was what you got. I liked that. I respected that.

My mom and my stepdad started dating right after the New Year's party. The three of us moved in together a few months later. I was excited when we went to look for new apartments together. The three of us were going to be a nuclear family. I never had one of those before. We found a nice, quaint, small apartment in Alborada. Alborada was a decent middle-class neighborhood of Guayaquil, if Guayaquil actually had a middle class. I spent a lot of time at the neighbor's house watching the Spanish version of *Batman* along with *El Chavo del Ocho* reruns, as my parents worked their long shifts at the hospital. They usually scheduled their hours so one of them could stay with me at night. If you had money in Ecuador, you would pay a maid to raise your children. My parents did not have that kind of money. Only private doctors who had the investment capital (i.e., family money) to start a private practice in Ecuador made that kind of money. Public doctors were at the mercy of Ecuadorian bureaucrats and the state of the national economy.

One night, my mom was working the graveyard shift. I was alone with my stepdad in the apartment when he got an emergency call around 11:30 p.m. A little girl had accidentally been shot with a shotgun from behind, and the hospital needed my stepdad—as the head surgeon—to lead the very complicated surgery. Without a second thought, my stepdad told me to put my shoes on and rushed us both out of the house. We arrived at the children's hospital in Guayaquil within twenty-five minutes. My stepdad handed me off to a nurse, who was waiting for us out front. My stepdad rushed in the opposite direction I did, as I followed the nurse to a nearby locker room. I didn't know what was happening. The nurse helped me undress and started putting oversize scrubs on my tiny body. She covered my mouth with an operating mask and placed disposable shoe covers on my feet. She walked me down a bright hallway. Everything felt so big: the neon lights, the corridor, the cold tile floor. We entered a restricted area and stopped to let a surgical assistant run past. The nurse then opened the large operating room door and gently pushed me inside.

Alone, I looked around the operating room. There was what appeared to be a spotlight directly in front of me. It illuminated a surgical bed, where I could make out a few figures hunched over it. I slowly walked toward it and realized they were a bunch of adults in scrubs and medical masks and in the bed lay a child. I could hear my stepdad. I knew he was the man ordering everyone around because of his signature Coke bottle glasses over his surgical mask. I looked over at the person administering the anesthesia and instinctively recognized my mom's kind eyes. I knew she was smiling at me despite her mouth being covered by the surgical mask. She was smizing before Tyra Banks could even coin the term! Then I looked at the patient. She was a little girl. Six years old. My age. Her chest was fractured and held open by four large steel tongs. I could see her organs pumping to stay alive. My dad was working as fast as he could to ensure she remained so. This entire event could have been a traumatic experience for me, but it wasn't because my parents were there. I was not scared. I was not disgusted. I was simply amazed. My parents were working frantically to save a child's life, and because they did not have any money for child care themselves, I was there to witness the entire thing. The whole experience, from where I was standing, felt like twenty minutes. Many years later, my mom laughed, remembering how I stood in that OR for seven hours with no break through one of the most complicated surgeries she and my stepdad ever tackled together. The little girl survived. In my eyes, my parents were real-life superheroes.

My stepdad and I had become close in such a short period of time, but we were close in the same way that a drill sergeant is with a new recruit. Like in the OR, my dad was used to barking orders, and as a young child, I was good at following them. There was never any leisure time with him. He was not the type of dad who would take you to a soccer game. He was the type of dad that mostly complained about why soccer players did not have real jobs. So it surprised me when he invited me to the movies one day. It turned out, my stepdad loved American films just as much as I did. Opening this particular weekend: *American Ninja*. You already know how this movie changed my life. But what you do not know is that my real dad never took me to the movies. In fact, I had started seeing him less and less in those days. As it was, Ronald was only a part-time dad, but with my stepdad around, he made a point to distance himself even more. Perhaps he was too busy with his blossoming law career. Perhaps he was trying to send my mom a message. For this exact reason, I looked over at my stepdad as he drove and asked, "Can I call you dad?" My stepdad looked over at me with the same austere look I had grown accustomed to. I could see my hopeful face reflected back at me in his thick lenses. He looked back at the road and simply replied, "Yes." I was ecstatic to finally have a full-time dad. I never called him my "stepdad" again.

One morning, I asked my mom if she could please buy me a ninja costume. I still reserved a special place in my heart for *Batman*, but *American Ninja* was on a whole other level. My mom was uncharacteristically silent that morning as she looked out our small kitchen window. I shrugged it off and went back to eating my fruit salad, knowing that I could always beg my grandma or her maid to sew me one. After a few moments, my mom turned to me and asked, "How would you like to live in America?" I stared up at my mom and wondered if she was serious. She smiled, relieved to finally share what she had been holding on to this whole time. I took a deep breath. Forget the costume, I was about to be a real American! I finished my mangos with visions of the American flag adorned with ninja stars dancing through my head.

It turned out my aunt Teresa, my mom's oldest sister who had been living in the States since I was born, had petitioned for us to come to America via the family reunification program. My parents were excited by the prospect of becoming doctors in the United States and making a good living at it. It seemed that all you needed to get ahead in the States was to be good at your job and be willing to work long, hard hours. In Guayaquil, a city nearly five hundred years old that was founded and looted by Spanish conquistadors, English and French pirates, and international merchants alike, you had to be slicker and more opportunistic than my parents ever cared to be. The United States seemed like a good change of pace for them. This country's family reunification program, by the way, is something we are familiar with today as "chain migration," a disparaging term that gained popularity when it became more closely associated with Black and brown people. Nobody seemed to care when the immigrants arriving on American shores were Northwestern European. Since Congress restricted naturalized citizenship to "white persons" in 1790, and then passed the Chinese Exclusion Act of 1882, as the first general immigration law in the United States, measures (i.e., quotas) restricting immigration from Asia, Africa, and Latin America have been long-standing in the land of liberty. Talentless landscape artist Adolf Hitler wrote about his admiration for the American immigration system by marveling: "The American Union categorically refuses the immigration of physically unhealthy elements, and simply excludes the immigration of certain races." With that frightening cheerleader of the American immigration system, and on the heels of the 1964 Civil Rights Act, the United States' immigration quota approach was rightfully attacked for being racially discriminatory. And in 1965, family reunification became the basis for the reform legislation that allowed my parents and me to come to this country.

In the following weeks there were a lot of international calls with my aunt Teresa. My mom had a revolving door of in-person conversations with my grandparents, my uncles, and my aunts. My grandfather looked particularly sad to lose his daughter to the Yankees. He was very solemn. I'm sure he was sad to lose me as well. The two of us had been inseparable since my birth. To me, he was "Tata," which was the noise I made as an infant when I first saw him: "ta-ta." Tata was one of the first people to move into Urdesa, the town I grew up in, and was a Supreme Court justice for all of Babahoyo, which is the equivalent of a California State Supreme Court justice if the California State Supreme Court were run by a bunch of drunken Ecuadorians. My grandma loves to tell the story of the time when I was three years old and I protected Tata from her wrath. My grandfather had come home drunk one night and she was furiously confronting him about it when out of nowhere I ran in between them, pushed her away, and said, "Leave my Tata alone!" She was still angry, but being shoved by a three-year-old boy made her laugh, and she had to leave the room to compose herself. Moments later, she came back with my mom, and the two of them could not believe that my grandfather and I were jabbering nonsense to each other, deep in conversation—confident that the other knew what we were each saying.

I was torn over how to feel about moving to America. I did not want to leave my grandparents, but I did want to live there. I had dreamed about becoming an American ever since I saw Rambo tie that red bandanna around his head. And the bonus was I would get to see my aunts and uncles and meet all my cousins, some of whom were my own age! I could not wait to play cops and robbers with them, but the American version, which I assumed was just a constant police state from the American action movies I watched. That's when my mom pulled me aside and whispered, "But you can't tell your father." She added poignantly, "This has to be our secret, or else he won't let you go."

My biological father would pick me up from time to time

and take me out with my other half siblings. I was the youngest of his four children. We were not close, but I knew I was special to him because I was the only one of his children who looked like him. To him, this was important because he grew up not looking like anybody in his family and he was treated differently than his siblings as a result. His earliest memories as a child were of his dad pushing him away when he asked for a hug, and he was eventually sent to live with his aunt and uncle at a large hacienda far away from the city. His uncle, Rafael, who I am named after, became his real father figure. Years later, when my biological father was in his mid-twenties and opening his first law practice, a stranger walked through his new office door and announced himself as *his* biological father. In an instant, everything made sense. He was the by-product of an affair.

I felt uncomfortable not telling the man who had given me life that I was leaving the country. My mom taught me never to lie, but then here she was asking me to keep this major secret from him. I felt anxious around my biological father. I tried not to speak unless spoken to. He figured I was having a bad time with him so he bought me some yogurt and yuca bread, and then dropped me back off with my mom shortly thereafter. I let out a big sigh of relief when I got home. I ate my yuca bread and wondered if the American yuca bread tasted as delicious. Spoiler alert: there is no yuca bread in the States! When would I have yuca bread again? When would I see my grandparents again? Was Gotham City even a real place? I questioned if I even wanted to leave Ecuador at all. I started to realize that life was pretty good for me in the middle of the world. Not only did my grandma have maids that could cook for me whenever I was hungry, but my grandfather was a big deal in Guayaquil. His brother was an admiral for the president of the Republic, which meant that my Tata had a lot of *palanca*. There was no real need to leave my posh Ecuadorian existence for the uncertainty of the United States. Would there even be maids for us in the States? Did my grandfather have any connections to the president of the United States? And what about this damn yuca bread!

We gave up our apartment in Alborada and went back to my grandparents' house for a few days. My mom bade farewell to my dad, who was packed for the long trip. He was going to the United States before us to try to get us situated. Time was clearly running out for me to voice any concerns. I didn't even have time to say bye to my friends, either. If the Irish Goodbye was when someone left a party without saying bye, then the Ecuadorian Good-bye was clearly when someone left the country without saying bye! Once my dad had left, my mom and I found ourselves alone in our old room—the same room that all my aunts and uncles had once called home. I told her, "I don't want to go to America anymore. I want to stay in Ecuador."

My mom looked at me warmly, taking in my concern. She then replied, "We're only going for a few months."

Fully convinced that we'd be back in no time, I happily started packing my bags for our American vacation. My mom folded up my Batman costume and started to place it in my suitcase, but I stopped her. "It's okay, we don't have to take it. It'll still be here when we get back." Secretly, I wanted my mom to buy me a ninja costume on our trip, but I didn't want her to know that.

We came to the United States the week of the Fourth of July weekend in 1988. My dad actually arrived on the Fourth of July itself. I know it sounds like I'm saying that for literary effect, but it's true! My dad arrived early to connect with his cousin who was living in LA County at the time. His cousin had come to Los Angeles, married a Filipina American for papers, got caught by immigration officials for lying, and ended up falling in love with the Filipina American anyway. How did they get caught? The immigration officials separated them during their home interview and asked each of them what kind of underwear my dad's cousin wore. She said, "Boxers." He said, "Briefs." That's why I always go commando!

My mom and I arrived in Los Angeles on a Friday night. As I sat next to her on the plane looking out at all the Fourth of July fireworks lighting up the LA night sky, I was convinced that they were there to announce our arrival. Little did I know that this was no vacation, and that this flight was really a one-way trip. To this day when I see Fourth of July fireworks, I envision an excited but clueless little ethnic kid on a plane thinking that the celebration is all for them.

My parents and I arrived in America with only five hundred dollars in our pockets. It was really in my dad's pockets, but what was mine was his and what was his could barely afford one month's rent. Once in Los Angeles, we moved in with my aunt Teresa and her husband, Sergio. Aunt Teresa and Uncle Sergio lived in a California ranch-style home in Walnut, California, with their three young children and a toy dog named Pacha, and they had a guest room in their garage that was meant to be our new residence. For me, this was like entering the Twilight Zone. Where was the red carpet announcing my arrival? Where were the maids to help us get settled in? Where was our freshly baked yuca bread? I didn't get it. Why were we constantly downgrading our living conditions? We went from a large house in Urdesa, to a small apartment in Alborada, to a literal garage in Los Angeles. *Luckily,* I thought, *this is just a vacation.*

My aunt Teresa was my mom's oldest sister and my godmother. Fun fact: Aunt Teresa was not present during my infant baptism because she was already living in the United States at the time, which officially makes her the first woman ever to stand me up. Aunt Teresa was a former beauty queen and a current mechanical engineer at McDonnell Douglas, a major American aerospace manufacturing corporation and defense contractor. My aunt Teresa's garage guest room could have seemed like a makeshift sauna that smelled of Armor All and Castrol GTX, but it didn't to us because it was our new home. More important, it didn't to me because I did not have to live in it. I was allowed to stay in my cousin Chochis's room inside the house. Chochis was two years younger than me, born one day after me in the same month, and by the unwritten laws of the immigrant family hierarchy, he was forced to look up to me. At least I liked to remind him of this as he ignored me and played his Nintendo by himself.

My aunt Teresa loved American animated films, which I did as well shortly after coming to the States. Like all children, I loved Sunday-morning cartoons, but animated films were another magical experience entirely. These weren't ongoing episodic stories. They were confined to a time and place, which made them that much more special—and easier to collect. That is why one unexpected night, she had us all sit down as a family to watch *An American Tail*. If you are a young immigrant to the United States and have never seen *An American Tail*, don't! Directed by Don Bluth and produced by Steven Spielberg, this sweeping animated feature film about a young Russian mouse that migrates to America with his family and subsequently loses them along the way, fucked me up. I cried that night in fear that I, too, would be separated from my parents in this country. Why would anybody show this traumatizing piece of family separation propaganda to a seven-year-old boy a few weeks after arriving in the United States? My aunt Teresa and Steven Spielberg owe me money for all the years of therapy that film caused me. Luckily, I can play "Somewhere Out There" to this day and happily cry myself to sleep at night.

The garage guest room eventually got a new twenty-inch color TV. This high-tech entertainment system was only possible because of my dad's new American job, which his cousin got for him. My dad's job was not at a hospital, but still I found it strange that he left for work not wearing his medical scrubs.

Up to that point, I figured every adult wore medical scrubs to go to work since that was what both my mom and my dad wore in Ecuador when they left the house. But becoming doctors in the States was not going to be easy. They discovered the hard way their medical licenses meant nothing in this country. They were forced to start from scratch. But that was not going to stop them. They were determined to work their way back to becoming doctors, even if it meant learning a new language, going back to school, and retaking the medical exam. But first, my dad left for his first day of work dressed in old blue jeans and an oversize white T-shirt. My dad's appearance is best described as "poor man's chic." Thanks to his cousin, my dad put his pediatric surgeon's hands to work on brand-new 1988 Nissan Maximas. Not on their engines, but on their wax detail. True to California immigrant tradition, my dad's first job in this country was at a car wash—the Alamo Car Wash in West Covina to be exact. The sad thing was that my dad made more money in tips at the car wash than he ever did saving children's lives in Ecuador, where he would more often than not be paid with live hens.

My mom, however, was shockingly close to hitting the jackpot. At least in my humble opinion. As I sat with her trying to translate the classified job listings in the newspaper, I saw that Pizza Hut was hiring. It dawned on me that if I could get my mom to work at Pizza Hut, then we could eat pizza every night. Let me explain: At the time, Pizza Hut was considered fine dining in Ecuador. Globally, fast-food companies don't change their prices. So given the standard of living in Ecuador, you could afford a plate of meat, rice, and beans for three dollars in 1988, but you could not afford a Quarter Pounder, let alone the cheese. In my eyes, if my mom got a job at Pizza Hut, it would be a boon to our social status. I encouraged her to apply every chance I got. Unfortunately, my mom did not agree with corporate America's nutritional standard of living, so Pizza Hut was a nonstarter with her. I was condemned to eating delicious and laboriously prepared Ecuadorian food at the risk of being seen as lower class by our new American neighbors, since we clearly did not have the kind of high salaries it required to afford pizza on a daily basis.

I eventually got to meet the rest of my extended family. My uncle Ivan, my mom's older brother and the reigning champ of all Spanish language dad jokes; his lovely Mexican wife, Lucha; and their three kids. Three kids seemed to be the going rate for Ecuadorian Americans in Los Angeles. As luck would have it, one of my uncle Ivan's kids, Choli, was my exact age. Choli and I became best friends from the moment we met. There was no small talk between us. We just ran outside and started playing basketball. As a soccer-prone South American kid, I didn't know how to shoot a basketball, but Choli took the time to teach me. It was amazing to have a cousin my exact age. It felt like finding a long-lost brother, except one of us could speak perfect English. One of our favorite pastimes was acting out Hollywood films in front of my aunt Teresa's living room TV. Our go-to was always John Travolta's *Grease*. I would play Danny Zuko, Choli would play Kenickie, his sister Diane would play Rizzo, Chochis's older sister Jessica would play Sandy, and Chochis himself would be forced to play all the other supporting characters. I wish I could say we knew how to perform the whole movie, but really we just rewound "Summer Nights" over and over again. It was a wonderful out-of-tune ethnic production that no adult in our family ever had time to watch.

A quick point of clarification: I didn't know I was seen as ethnic at the time. Please understand that at this early stage of my life I didn't know what ethnicity was. I had never heard the term "Latino" or "Hispanic" in Ecuador. My cousin Choli had light skin and blue eyes, for crying out loud! What was my elementary school brain to make of all this? I was a privileged little white kid (with a beautiful olive tan) in South America, so to me, everyone was either rich (white) or poor (people who couldn't afford pizza).

As much as I was having fun with my cousins, I looked forward to going back to be with my grandparents. Like most kids in Latin America, I was essentially raised by Grandma and Grandpa. I missed them terribly. I figured my parents and I would head back to see them real soon. Then my birthday came, and my mom made the biggest mistake of her young adult life. She conspired with my aunt Teresa to celebrate Chochis's and my birthday on the same day as a way to save money and not have to overspend on two parties. I had no idea this terrible plan was hatched. My mom said we were going to Chuck E. Cheese for my birthday and I took her at face value. I did find it odd when I saw some of Chochis's younger friends at Chuck E. Cheese with us, but I assumed they just wanted to celebrate my life. Back in Guayaquil, my birthdays were *the* thing to do. My grandfather would use it as an excuse to throw a big party and invite the whole town. One year, he rented an electric train to take me and all the neighborhood kids around the block. In other words, as far as I was concerned, my birthday was *my day* and nobody else's. That was the attitude I carried when the birthday cake finally came out and I saw both Chochis's and my names written on it. *Oh hell no.* When everyone sang "Happy Birthday," I went out of my way to repeat "Rafa" twice so that it sounded like: "Happy Birthday to you. Happy Birthday to you. Happy Birthday Rafa and . . . RAFA!" My grandma would have never allowed this travesty to occur. To this day, Chochis and I still have not recovered.

If birthday parties were going to be like this in America, then I wanted no part of it. American Ninja didn't have to celebrate his birthday with other ninjas, but then again I didn't see his birthday in the film. In any case, I immediately asked my mom when we were going back to Ecuador. She said, "Soon." I asked her a week later, and she said, "Soon." She repeated the lie so often that I stopped believing her, and one day I just started to cry. I was disheartened. I missed my friends. I missed my grandparents. Chochis was no longer talking to me because I had refused to acknowledge his birth. This entire vacation was starting to feel like a debacle. That's when my mom leveled with me . . .

"We came here to start a new life. Your dad and I are going

to school to learn English, so that we can both become doctors here. And you're going to go to school here, too."

My mom had misled me. She had never lied to me before that moment, so this was a lot to take in. On the one hand, the way my mom spoke to me as an adult at eight years of age was very sobering. On the other hand, she had lied—and she taught me never to lie. Ultimately, this country made my mom lie to me, which meant America and I now had ourselves a problem! I decided to toughen up. No more nice little Ecuadorian boy. It was time for me to grow up and adapt. Charles Darwin developed his theory of evolution in Ecuador—in the Galápagos Islands—so the least I could do was try to adapt to my new surroundings. I learned to use a microwave. I also learned to take out the trash. I needed to stop acting like a privileged little white South American kid. I stopped complaining that there were no chauffeurs to take us to the park. Walk to the park? No problem. I was no longer insulted by my aunt Teresa's suggestion. I even stopped resenting the garage guest room for its lack of amenities. Everything seemed to be going great until I attended my first day of public school.

Up to that point in my life, I had only been enrolled in private schools. Catholic guilt, hideous school uniforms, and a lack of diversity were what I had grown accustomed to. I assumed American public schools would be the same. My mom and I arrived at Oswalt Elementary at 7:30 a.m. on a Monday morning. As all the white kids ran past us screaming in English, it became clear to me that I would be the only white kid at school who did not speak the language. Luckily, my cousin Choli was already attending Oswalt Elementary, so I was going to have someone to hang out with at recess. That was when I saw a few African American kids run by. Then some Asian American kids. I had never seen this much diversity in one place in my life. It was overwhelming. The American film and TV shows I watched growing up did not have this many minorities in them. Perceiving them as danger, my inner Michael Dudikoff wanted to come out and defend America for some reason. And then I saw them: the Mexican American kids. And by God, they looked more like me than I did the white kids. This truth was hard to comprehend. I was about to have a brain aneurysm.

My mom walked me over to the front office. As she finalized my student paperwork, my mother stumbled onto a question she had never seen before. The question asked: "Is your child a special student?" Well, my mother, not knowing that "special" had a double meaning in English, and knowing that I was on the honor roll at my previous school, and—let's face it—since I was an only child, of course my mother considered me to be pretty damn special, she wrote: "Yes. Mi hijo is a special student."

Needless to say, on my first week of school in this great nation, I was placed in special education classes. From the beginning I sensed there was something off about my new lessons. Granted I didn't have a complete grasp of the English language but I knew something was terribly wrong when the teacher stood in front of our third-grade class with one orange in her right hand and one orange in her left and proceeded to say, "One orange plus one orange equals two oranges." It's not just that I thought it was a little offensive to be teaching an immigrant child with oranges! I was more befuddled. Were all the kids in this class "special" or did we just not speak English? I tried to communicate with my blond teacher that I was three levels more advanced in math and science than my entire grade, but she didn't know what I was saying. They pulled my poor cousin Choli out of class so he could translate for me. Choli walked into my class completely embarrassed to be associated with the one non–English speaker. His Kenickie swagger had all but disappeared. He translated what I said to my teacher: "Ms. Summers, I don't belong in this class." Ms. Summers let out an audible *aww*, and then chimed in: "I know. Nobody does." Choli went back to his class, and I went back to my seat, confused.

On the work front, a family friend had told my dad about a clinical job at Good Samaritan Hospital in downtown Los Angeles. It was for a technician position at their sleep disorder center. My dad was overqualified with his background, but at that point, my dad would have taken any job that would get him out of hand washing any more automobiles. The new job required a social security number. Luckily, when they arrived in the States, my aunts and uncles explained to my parents that they would need social security numbers as adults. It would allow them to work and drive in the country, so they were able to get theirs before laws on who was able to acquire a social security number changed. My parents, however, did not get me a social security card because, according to everyone's logic, I was a child and was not going to work anytime soon. Why would I need a social security number? More on that later.

My dad got hired at the sleep disorder center, which meant he could leave the car wash work in his rearview mirror. Because my dad's new job required him to stay up late at night while his patients were asleep, my mom would accompany him while my dad monitored the brain waves of his patients. His new employers didn't know my mom was there, but it was the graveyard shift and there was nobody around to say anything. My mom was really there for moral support. My dad was in a new country, in a new job, and barely knew the language. My mom's presence calmed him a great deal.

This was my parents' routine that first year in this country: attend Mt. San Antonio College for English as a Second Language classes during the day and then head over to the Good Samaritan for the graveyard shift. I rarely saw them. I would stay up late at night wondering where they were. Their absence, ironically, gave me a sleep disorder! I thought the whole point was to come to America for a better life. Things seemed to be worse here than they were in Ecuador.

With my mom accompanying my dad to work every evening, my parents and I were like ships in the night. We would see each other in the mornings, but then not again until the weekends. I spent most of my nonschool hours with my cousins, while the adults in the house all worked full-time. By the time the weekend rolled around, everyone seemed exhausted—my parents most of all. America was a different way of life and they were barely getting accustomed to it. In Ecuador, not everybody had the privilege of finding work, but at least everyone made time to be with their families. Maybe it was because of all the free time they had from not working!? In the States, however, any capable body could find menial work, and you could keep that work for as long as you were able to produce. Unfortunately, there was no real time for family in this country.

If my mom regretted coming to America, she never showed it. She took on this new tiring experiment for her husband and son, and she never once complained about it. My dad said they would be doctors in America one day, maybe even at UCLA Medical, and by God, she believed him. They both worked tirelessly toward that goal. First Monday through Friday, but eventually seven days a week. It's heartbreaking to think that they were never able to become doctors in the United States. Because the greatest lesson my parents ever learned in this country was that the American Dream is not for you, but for your children.

Field of Dreams

My parents eventually saved enough money to move us out of the garage and into our first tiny apartment in Duarte, California. It was not as nice as the apartment we'd had in Ecuador, but it was a step in the right direction. The apartment complex was next to a freeway, a bit rundown, and full of minority families. Funny enough, I was starting to understand that, in this country, my fate was more intertwined with minority families than with any white person I idolized in the American films I always loved.

The year was 1989. I said bye to all my cousins and Oswalt Elementary, and we moved to Duarte to live close to my mom's cousins, my aunt Betty, and my uncle Pete. I had never met them before coming to the States, but like all my American relatives, they were very welcoming. Duarte felt like a nice, quiet little conservative town. I was excited. In my head, we were finally going to live our vision of Americana. The large electrical cables and transmission towers around the neighborhood were dampening our perfect American painting, but you got the idea.

At that time, my parents were fighting to stay in front of their vastly accumulating debt after getting the apartment and a new used car. They were shocked by how eager credit card companies were to preapprove them for new lines of credit. Unfortunately, financial literacy is not anything they teach you once you cross through customs. My mom received her first credit card in Ecuador only after proving she had several years of work under her belt. In the United States, she received a credit card without ever having a job. I noticed that my dad started to have anxiety over money around this time. Getting bills in the mail was a surefire way to ruin his day.

One day, my dad received an unexpected flyer in the mail. I was just grateful it wasn't another bill. It was a flyer from a local nonprofit apparently trying to help immigrant workers. The flyer was intended to provide some financial literacy to the surrounding immigrant communities. I helped my dad translate it: "If you want to make it in this economy, you need to keep two jobs at all times to ensure you can survive a recession." That's all my dad needed to hear. He started looking for a second job immediately. He had the sleep center job Monday through Friday, and found part-time work doing medical reports for clinics Saturdays and Sundays. I never saw my dad again. Except for our ampm Sunday trips, of course.

ampm was a chain of convenience stores on the West Coast, not unlike 7-Eleven, that also sold fast food. They were always attached to gas stations. My dad insisted on taking my mom and me out on Sundays to ampm for hamburgers. In those days, I couldn't care less about the eating ambience. ampm was a phenomenal experience for me because it was my first exposure to Heinz Ketchup. Why didn't anybody tell me how good America tasted? I almost signed up to canvass for John Kerry's presidential campaign after I learned he married into the Heinz family. I am certain Heinz puts crack (the same drug as cocaine, but with harsher sentences for people of color) in their ketchup. In other words, Heinz Ketchup tasted remarkable on my Sunday ampm hamburger. I was completely clueless that my dad took us there because he could not afford more than the "ninety-nine cents for two hamburgers" promotion that ampm had at the time. ampm was how my dad fed his family on Sundays, and you know what? I loved it. I would not trade any expensive meal today for the memory of eating a fifty-cent hamburger at a gas station with my mom and dad. Many years later, my dad shared with me that his lowest point in this country was having to take my mom and me to ampm for dinner. Crazy . . . that was the highlight of my childhood.

Shortly after moving to Duarte, my anesthesiologist mom was finally able to land her first American job. I had been inside a Kmart only once before. I remember thinking it was way too big. Ecuador didn't have bargain stores the size of Kmart. Every aisle looked vast and endless. I feared I would get lost forever. I stayed close to my mom at the time because I felt this was the kind of store that swallowed little children. Our local Kmart was not close and my parents had only one car between them, so since my dad had to drive the farthest, my mom volunteered to walk an hour to get to the outskirts of town where her new employer resided. After her first day of American employment, my mom came home and told my dad and me that she had found something interesting on the Kmart floor. She had found two lonely hundred-dollar bills miraculously waiting there for her. Two Benjamins were not nothing to a newly arrived immigrant desperate to start making cash to provide for her family. But as opposed to pocketing the money and buying her well-behaved, angelic child a much-deserved G.I. Joe action set equipped with its own army Humvee vehicle, my mom turned in the two hundred dollars to her supervisors. My dad thought she had done the right thing, although I could tell by the tone of his voice that he would have pocketed the money. The next day, my mom discovered through her Spanish-speaking coworkers that the two hundred dollars on the floor was a trick that local Kmart management played on new employees to see how honest they were. This, of course, was pretty disgusting, but it did not seem to faze my mom. She proudly shared this story with us as we ate the Chef Boyardee can of raviolis she'd brought home from work. If God was indeed testing her character, my mom felt like she was passing with flying colors. I'm not sure if they implemented that two hundred-dollar-bill policy at all minority-heavy Kmart stores, but regardless, my mom would have turned that money in.

My mom got into her groove at work. All her Spanish-speaking coworkers loved her cheerful demeanor. She even liked the long walk home. She thought it kept her fit. One evening, however, as my mom made her way back to our apartment, she glanced across the street and saw a white man of roughly her same age coming out of a real estate office. At first she didn't think anything of it—the man was wearing a suit and wasn't very remarkable. But then he smirked at my mom, unzipped his pants, and exposed himself—he couldn't care less who was around to see. Fearing she would be assaulted, my mom ran. Panting and almost completely out of breath, she headed toward the first restaurant she saw. Luckily, it was a Mexican restaurant. She felt safe. In Spanish, she told the host what had happened and they allowed her to use their phone. My mom did not call the police. Calling the police was more frightening than a strange man holding his dick in his hand. The host and a few servers went outside to confront the man, but he had since disappeared. My dad had no choice but to buy a second car. He didn't know how they were going to afford it, but he could not let my mom walk home from work anymore.

My mom now had a new used car, and the two of us used it whenever she wasn't working. Mostly to go visit my aunts, uncles, and cousins who did not live near Duarte. The car was a bit of a jalopy, but it got us from point A to point B. One day, when my mom and I were driving home from a faraway aunt's house, the car broke down on the rough, industrial side of town. We weren't even halfway to point B. My mom and I were alone, but we managed to push the car to a nearby mechanic, who needed to keep the vehicle overnight. I stood next to my mom at a corner pay phone as she called my dad and all my aunts and uncles with the few quarters she had in her cupholder in hopes that someone could pick us up. Nobody could. My mom hung up the pay phone, and with no rideshare apps for another twenty years, she grabbed my hand and said, "We're walking home." I was a little concerned because of the shady neighborhood we were in, but I looked up at my mom and she showed no fear, so I felt safe.

We started our long trek home from the auto repair shop. We walked through dirty streets, past seedy bars, by some warehouses, and across a long freeway overpass. Cars would slow down as they drove past us. I could hear the men catcalling my beautiful, petite mother, but I was never scared, because every time I looked up at her, she showed no fear. She was determined to get us home safe.

After a while, my feet started to hurt from all the walking. I was very tired and asked if we were almost home. My mom said, "Almost." Twenty minutes passed and I asked her the same question. Again, she responded, "Almost." We walked for over four hours that day. We made it home to Duarte at dusk. My dad got home roughly around the same time. He was so worried for my mom and me that his fear had turned into irritation. "I can't believe no one in your family could pick you up," he said, upset that nobody in my mom's large family could give us a ride home. But to be fair, neither did he.

Between all the canned food during the week and all the ampm burgers on the weekends, I was starting to gain a lot of weight in this country. Canned food, fast food, processed food—I had never been this cruel to my body. If my mom would buy an international calling card to call my grandparents, I would grab the phone and declare with glee, "Grandma—I'm fat now!" People could not believe how much weight I had gained. I was always a skinny kid in Ecuador. Maybe it was the equatorial sun that made me sweat a lot, or perhaps it was the homemade food that was healthier for my tiny body. Whatever the case, my waistline was expanding faster than American Imperialism. It was time for me to join a sport.

As you may have guessed, my aunt Betty and my uncle Pete had three Ecuadorian American children of their own. The oldest, my cousin Raul, was one year older than me and was obsessed with baseball. This meant that I, in turn, started to get obsessed with baseball as well. Besides, baseball was America's pastime! We mostly played soccer in Ecuador, but there was too much running and athleticism required for *fútbol*. Baseball. Now there was a less-tiring sport I could get behind. You hit the ball as hard as you could three or four times a game, stood in the same spot in the outfield for hours on end waiting for something to happen, and you ate a lot of hot dogs after the game. Baseball was definitely the sport for me.

Raul and I would play baseball at the park near his house all day and would stop only to watch the televised Dodgers games. We were still hot off the Dodgers '88 World Series win a year earlier. And if you recall, 1988 was the year I arrived in this country. People can argue that Babe Ruth (was he Black?) or Jackie Robinson (definitely Black) or Ted Williams (half

Mexican!) were better baseball players. But to me, the greatest player ever to pick up a bat will forever be Kirk Gibson. Gibson was not supposed to have an at bat in game one of the '88 MLB World Series, and was out of that crucial first game against the highly favored Oakland A's due to two knee injuries. Nevertheless, with no other options and the tying run in scoring position at the bottom of the ninth inning, Gibson hobbled out of the dugout and onto the batter's box to a deafening stadium's surprise. I watched the game with my cousins glued to the TV. The count got to three balls, two strikes. A full count. What happened next is baseball legend. Now imagine watching that World Series at bat as a newly arrived immigrant boy in Los Angeles. When Hall of Fame announcer Vin Scully called that game-winning home run, he might as well have been talking about me coming to America: "In a year that has been so improbable, the impossible has happened!" Kirk Gibson never had to have another at bat again. That home run will forever be the welcome to this country that I needed.

Raul had one actual valuable possession displayed on his shelf that he had gotten a year before I had moved to Duarte. It was a baseball signed by former Dodger Steve Garvey. Garvey was by then a retired first baseman that was a ten-time All-Star, a past National League Most Valuable Player winner, and held the National League record for most consecutive games played. That is a work ethic any immigrant parent could admire! Raul explained to me that he got to meet him at a Dodgers game he attended with his Little League team. Curious, I asked, "That's all you have to do to meet the Dodgers?

Just join Little League?" Raul confidently nodded his head. I begged my mom to sign me up for Little League that same night. It was the only way I could ever meet the Dodgers, since I knew my parents could not afford taking me to an actual game. My mom said she would look into it. As long as it was not too expensive, she would sign me up.

A few weeks later, Raul was invited to another Dodgers game with his Little League team. I was incredibly jealous, but I could not wait for Raul to get back home and tell me all about his experience at Dodger Stadium. I needed to know what the players looked like in person. Did he catch any foul balls? Did Kirk Gibson ask about me? As soon as Raul got home, I begged my mom to drive me to his house. I ran in, gave my aunt and uncle their mandatory kisses on the cheek, and sprinted to Raul's bedroom. I bombarded him with a million questions. Raul smiled with the poise of a media mogul talking to an aspiring journalist desperate for a big break. Not only did he watch the whole game in person, but he also got to see the players warm up. Manager Tommy Lasorda even waved at him. In my opinion, Raul could have died a happy kid at that point. What else did he need to live for? Raul then pulled out a brand-new baseball signed by most of the Dodgers players. I was transfixed. I could not believe my very own cousin, a son of Ecuadorian immigrant parents, was able to get the Dodgers to acknowledge his existence, let alone sign his ball. Taking in my utter amazement, Raul then decided to do the nicest thing he had ever done for me, before or since: he gave me the other signed Dodgers baseball he owned. "Here," he said, handing me the ball inside its clear plastic case. "My signed Steve Garvey baseball. It's yours." Holy Shakira. I didn't know who Steve Garvey was at the time, but it didn't matter. He was a Dodger! I cradled that Steve Garvey autographed ball like an infant. On our drive home I showed my mom, but I would not allow her to touch it. Steve Garvey was no Kirk Gibson, but this signed Dodgers baseball still became my newest and most valuable possession in my room.

My dad was not into baseball. He grew up playing basketball in South America—a vertically challenged Ecuadorian sporting thick bottle-framed glasses in love with hoops. My dad lacked height, but he could shoot a mean jump shot. If you put black frames on John Stockton, that's exactly what my dad looked like in those days. That was probably why I never cheered for the Utah Jazz—every time they played, I felt like I was going to get grounded! My dad wasn't into baseball, but that didn't stop him from asking one Sunday morning, "Why don't we go to the park and play catch?" I forcefully rubbed my eyes to make sure I wasn't still dreaming. Was he serious? Playing catch with him was all I ever wanted to do.

My parents and I walked to Royal Oaks Park together. I was giddy beyond belief. I was nine and about to play America's pastime with my dad. I felt like I was in an episode of *Leave It to Beaver*, except that the sun was bright yellow and not black and white. My mom set up a picnic for us with the leftovers we had from the night before, while my dad did something he had never done—he put on a baseball glove. Maybe he had picked up on my love for the sport. Or maybe he felt bad that

42

we had never played catch in all of our time in the United States. Whatever the reason, this Sunday he was going to play catch with his son.

The first few throws were not bad. At least my dad was trying. I had better technique than he did from watching all the Orel Hershiser highlight reels, but he had the strength. My dad also had good hand-eye coordination. He had to as a pediatric surgeon—children's lives depended on it. I got so caught up playing catch with him that I nearly cried when I accidentally threw the ball over the wall and into someone's backyard. The wall was impossibly tall, and no matter how much I yelled, there didn't appear to be anybody home. Shit. It was the only baseball I had to play with. Why didn't I have another ball? This was a travesty. My dad felt terrible about the situation and asked, "What should we do?" My mind raced. The sports store was not close enough for us to go buy another ball. Who was I kidding? We didn't have the money for something as extravagant as a new baseball. Only our apartment was close, but I did not have spares. I had used them all with Raul. My dad tried to put me at ease by saying that we could come back and play catch next weekend, but I knew that was not going to happen. Playing catch with me was reserved for days he didn't have to go to work, which up to that point was exactly one day—that day!

Against my better judgment, I told my dad to hang tight and I raced home. As I ran full speed to our apartment, it dawned on me that this was all I ever wanted: to play baseball with my dad. I held on to the hope that I had a misplaced ball somewhere under my bed. I barged into my room, looked around everywhere—but nothing. Then I remembered: there was exactly one baseball left inside the apartment. I stared at the signed Dodgers ball still enclosed in its protective plastic case. It was either protect Steve Garvey forever or keep playing catch with my dad. The answer seemed clear.

I ran back to Royal Oaks Park yelling: "I found one! I found a ball!" My dad got up from my mom's picnic blanket, put his glove back on, and shouted—"Shoot it!" (I warned you he didn't know much about baseball.) I looked at the autographed ball in my hand. My most prized possession in this country. I'm not going to lie, that first throw was painful. I could feel the ink evaporating midair . . . the oxygen scraping against the ball. Then there was my dad's throw that was short and bounced off the grass. I winced. I could see the green of the grass grab on to the white of the ball. But as we continued playing, the joy I felt superseded any love I had for the entire Dodgers organization, Kirk Gibson notwithstanding. I laughed as I threw the ball as hard as I could and my dad pretended to have a hard time catching it. The California sun was shining bright on three Latin American immigrants that day.

Doctors with Borders

The week before I started my new school in Duarte, my mom asked me, "Do you want to go to Disneyland?" She already knew the damn answer. I had been begging her to take me since we got to this country. I was excited. I couldn't believe that after several years of begging we were finally going to Disneyland. My mom had scraped enough money together to make my wish come true. Disneyland was not anywhere near where we lived. It was in a different county altogether, but a trip to the most magical place on earth was a must. I couldn't sleep the night before. I kept wondering what Disneyland would be like and if all the characters I had seen in the Disney animated films would be there. My mom had read to me all the Disney stories in Ecuador and then subsequently shown me all the Disney movies in the United States. I was ready to meet Snow White, Mickey Mouse, Cinderella, Donald Duck, Sleeping Beauty, Goofy, etc. You name it, and I was ready for them!

The first step inside the park was breathtaking. There was

a train station welcoming us with a large Mickey Mouse head made of flowers directly in front of it. The monorail whizzed by us from on high. Inside the happiest place on earth (marketing really does work on me), I asked my mom to please buy me a blue Mickey Mouse T-shirt that I saw displayed in a gift shop's window. She regrettably said no because we did not have that kind of money. Bummed, I followed her to stand in line for a ride of a Disney character I had never heard of before. I asked my mom out loud: "Who is Peter Pan?" The American families around us gasped. "You never read Peter Pan to your son?" asked one randomly offended mother. "Peter Pan is an essential Disney character," exclaimed another. Everyone standing within a fifteen-foot radius demanded to know why my mom had never taught me anything about Peter Pan. Feeling mortified, my mom took me out of the line and we went straight to the gift shop to buy me the blue Mickey Mouse T-shirt instead. My mom feels great shame to this day for not having read Peter Pan to me at an earlier age. And quite frankly, she should.

Post Disney, I was finally ready to enter the fourth grade at Royal Oaks Elementary. This was yet another new start for me. I saw it as another chance to get this American student thing right. My previous school had been tough. It took me a full school year to properly learn English. If not for my cousin Choli, I would have been completely isolated. But now that I could speak English, it was easier for me to make friends. Like a lot of the schools I attended in those early years, Royal Oaks was filled with older white teachers trying to instruct a bunch of rowdy minority students. I was starting to feel at home within multicultural America.

I liked school in Duarte. There were a lot more immigrant and Latino kids. That made me feel like I was part of a family, it made me feel safer, and it helped me start my learning process. There was one girl in class, however, who really stood out: Erin. Erin was a white, freckle-faced nine-year-old with bright red hair and sparkling blue eyes. Ironically, Erin was exotic-looking in a sea full of kids of color. Like I mentioned before, I watched a lot of TV as a child and all the desirable people I saw on the screen were fair-skinned, so it's no wonder that shaped my sense of what made a person pretty. And I wasn't alone in idealizing this aesthetic. I watched the women in my life make themselves look more like these glamorous white Hollywood actresses. Even my beautiful darker-skinned aunts dyed their hair blond. As I look back on things now, I realize that it wasn't just Hollywood that promoted Eurocentric beauty. When my parents watched Spanish language television, all its stars, hosts, and news reporters were light-skinned and had light-colored eyes. I wasn't aware of the politics of it at the time, but I certainly internalized that standard of beauty. Erin was that standard personified.

I had admired Erin from afar for months. I rarely talked to her directly, but when I said something smart or funny in class, I was always hyperaware if she was paying attention. So I was taken off-guard when one of Erin's girlfriends approached me one morning during recess. This was also unusual since boys and girls were generally segregated—due to cooties and other deadly diseases. She asked me if I thought Erin was pretty. Without thinking, I said, "Yes, of course." The friend replied that Erin liked me, too, and that she would let her know. "Hold on," I said, without having any follow-up statement ready. It occurred to me that I shouldn't let someone I liked know that I liked them. But I had already shown my hand and I didn't know a cool way to walk it back. Erin's friend waited for me to say something but I didn't have anything to say. The friend shrugged, turned, and ran back to the girls' side of the playground to report her findings. Of course, for the rest of the afternoon I thought of all the things I could have said that would have made me seem mysterious and intriguing. But my fate was sealed and I would just have to wait it out.

Thankfully I didn't have to wait long. That evening, I was having dinner with my parents when the phone rang. Usually, when we received a call around this time, a family member was on the other end of the line. If we were lucky, it was an international call from my grandma to see how we were doing. My mom picked up the phone and said hello. She listened for a few seconds and then, bewildered, handed me the phone. "It's for you." Curious, I grabbed the phone and said hello in Spanish.

"Hi. It's Erin."

"Oh, hi."

There was an awkward beat between us. I had never spoken to a girl on the phone before. I didn't know what to say. Erin then complained about a kid in class that I thought was annoying, and we were off to the races. Erin and I spoke on the phone for roughly thirty minutes before I heard her mom demanding that she get off the landline. We were both nine years old, so we were really just talking about our friends and the classwork that we both hated. When I hung up, my mom asked, "Who was that?"

"A girl from school."

"A new friend?" she asked, her eyes twinkling with amusement that annoyed me.

"I guess."

My mom chuckled, knowing that I didn't know what I was getting myself into.

Erin and I waved at each other at school the next day, but that was it. At home that evening, Erin called me again. This became our routine. I have no idea why Erin liked me. I didn't even like myself, not since leaving Ecuador. I was chubby and spoke with an accent in the States. I didn't like girls. I just wanted to play baseball. Erin called my house every evening like clockwork. My parents couldn't believe it. If the phone was not ringing because of family, they always feared it would ring because of the landlord demanding his rent money. Instead, it rang because of Erin.

On one of our many evening calls, Erin finally asked, "Do you want to be my boyfriend?" I didn't know what that meant. Would being someone's boyfriend add more chores to my day? Confused and slightly weary, I still replied, "Sure." That reply would define my view on romantic relationships for the next twenty years. I always just went with the flow.

One pleasant Sunday, I rode my bike to Erin's house. This

was the first time we'd be together outside of school. Erin and her brothers were going to play Dungeons and Dragons, a board game I had never heard of before, and she thought it would be neat if I joined them. *Sure*, I thought. When I got there, I was surprised to discover she lived in an apartment building just like I did, yet I had never run into somebody that looked like Erin. I walked in and said hi to Erin, her mom, her grandma, and her two younger brothers I didn't even know existed, and we sat down to play the board game together at the dining room table. I was handed a character sheet that looked very puzzling. Then an elaborate map of the world was placed in front of us. It started to feel like they were giving me home-work on a Saturday, and I was not happy about that. After one of Erin's brothers pompously declared himself the Dungeon Master, the lead storyteller, and the rule maker, I completely checked out of the game. The only reason I did not leave was because I was Erin's boyfriend. And since I didn't really know what that meant, I thought it would be best if I just hung out with her and did what I was told. Another relationship lesson I wish I would have remembered as an adult! Erin had two brothers—both younger. And while it is supposedly Hispanics who have large families, there I was—an only child—hanging out with a white family that was bigger than mine. Perhaps they were Catholic as well.

My dad always complained about my mom's siblings. I didn't understand why until I played Dungeons and Dragons with Erin's brothers. They were annoyingly obsessed over the game and how to choose the proper race and class of your character. I remember thinking that maybe I didn't want Erin's younger brothers as in-laws, in the way that my dad didn't want my mom's siblings as in-laws. I don't know how I knew this at nine years of age, but the Dungeon Master struck me as the type of brother-in-law who would always be asking me for money.

After two excruciatingly long hours, I finally said good-bye to Erin and her family. I was glad to be done with Dungeons and Dragons forever. I walked outside and picked up my bike. Before I could pedal away, Erin rushed out and stood between my bicycle and the sidewalk. She smiled at me coquettishly, and then slowly leaned in. I didn't know what she was doing, or why she was leaning so close to my face. Erin closed her eyes. I wondered, *Was she trying to smell my shirt?* My mom was using a new fabric softener that smelled splendid, but how could Erin know that? I could barely smell it myself. Erin puckered her lips, stopped waiting for me to get a clue, and just went in for the kiss herself. I was stunned, but I did not complain. It was my first kiss. Not even a Dungeon Master could have written it any better.

While I was busy tangling with the Dungeon Master, my parents were on an adventure of their own. It started when they decided to take a walk around the neighborhood. When you don't have much money, long walks are the pastime of choice. In an outdoor strip mall next to our local gas station, my parents saw a sign they had never seen before. It was a poster of Uncle Sam pointing directly at them. This drawing of a chiseled man with a white top hat and blue jacket was calling my parents in. I did not know it at the time, but my parents and I had overstayed our tourist visas and we were in the country without documentation. That put us at great risk for deportation, and added a lot of stress to my mom and dad's daily work lives. They kept all this from me, allowing me to live the life of a normal American kid, but their anxiety about it haunted everything they did. That was why my parents thought that perhaps joining the United States military was the best way to rectify the immigration mess they found themselves in.

My mom and dad anxiously sat across from a military recruiter. He was a tall, clean-cut, African American officer. At the time, the United States desperately needed soldiers to enlist for Operation Desert Shield and Operation Desert Storm, and this military recruiter had just hit the jackpot with my medical doctor parents. On most days he was lucky to get a high school dropout or two to walk into his recruitment station, but standing there before him on this day were two adults in their prime—both doctors—and both willing to go to war for this country. "You are exactly what the military needs," exclaimed the recruiter as he picked up his telephone and started dialing. He wasted no time in calling his superior. My parents looked at each other; it was all happening so fast. There was so much hope and anticipation behind this one phone call, but would they check with immigration? Without saying anything to one another, it was clear that if they were going to get anywhere on this day, they would have to come clean. They steeled themselves and said: "We need to tell you that we do not have our immigration papers." The recruiter nodded his head and said, "Don't worry—we'll make this work." My parents looked at each other and smiled. For the first time since landing in this country, they finally let out a sigh of relief.

As hard as he tried, the recruiter could not get any of his superiors to sign off on my parents' enlistment. Their lack of immigration papers turned out to be more of a complication than he had ever imagined. It was now evening, but the recruiter was determined. He refused to let my parents leave— he even offered to buy them dinner. By this point, my parents had filled him in on everything: how they came to the country with tourist visas and then overstayed. He also knew they were a pediatric surgeon and an anesthesiologist living in the United States without proper work authorization. He knew that they would do anything to right that wrong, and that they were ready to go to the Middle East and serve as doctors on the front lines for this country to do so. The recruiter thought it was a no-brainer. He saw it as a fair trade: the United States did not have to invest any money in my parents' formal education and subsequent residencies to become doctors, yet would benefit fully from all of their medical expertise. But no matter how hard he tried, or how much he begged over the phone, he could not get any supervisor to sign off on my parents joining the service. That was the evening my parents learned their situation was impossible—no matter how well intentioned they were, there was no clear path to documentation and their son's future was at risk because of that. Defeated, the military recruiter apologized, said his final good-bye at the door, and felt worse than my parents did for not being able to enlist them in the United States Armed Forces.

My mom and dad arrived at our small apartment that evening feeling drained. Their concern over how long they would remain in this immigration limbo was taking a toll. They found me sitting on the couch watching TV. I had just had my first kiss—in this country or any other. My dad brought out his wallet and saw that he had only five dollars to his name. He looked up at me and asked, "Do you want to go to ampm?"

Oliver Stone's Office

I was a gigantic fan of American movies growing up, but I didn't realize people made a living doing them until I was nine years old and found myself roaming around Oliver Stone's house. And none of this would have been possible without my newest roommate, my uncle Javier.

My uncle Javier, my dad's younger brother, came to live with us when he first moved to the United States while we were in Duarte. This was by far the happiest I had seen my dad in a while. My uncle Javier was a tall, muscular, light-skinned Ecuadorian. Like my dad, he was of Italian and Asian descent. But unlike my dad, he got all the rugged good looks in the family. He came to the United States for one thing and one thing only: to work. It was funny seeing him try to get accustomed to the colloquial Mexican Spanish that dominated the Los Angeles labor force. On his first day of employment in LA, he got into a fistfight with a Mexican coworker because the guy said, *"Apurate, güey"* ("Hurry up, dude"), and my uncle understood, *"Apurate, buey"* ("Hurry up, ox"). My uncle's Mexican coworker ended up with a black eye for no apparent reason. It was all lost in cultural translation.

Because we lived in a two-bedroom apartment, my uncle Javier and I were forced to share a room. I didn't mind. He usually left for work before I had to head to school. And school was great for me at this time because I was able to make friends, and some even lived in the same apartment complex as me. My friends would come over after class, only to be shocked by my uncle's big muscles. My uncle was just out of military service and was ripped. When more and more kids around the apartment building showed up, I instinctively became a circus ringmaster. I didn't charge anybody, but I would walk them inside my house in pairs of two to show off my uncle. My uncle had no idea why I would parade elementary school kids inside our bedroom sporadically throughout the day, but I knew exactly what I was doing. My uncle was an impressive specimen, and I knew I would be considered impressive by association. Nobody needed to know that he was my step-uncle and that we did not share a bloodline.

My uncle Javier could not believe I had a girlfriend. He was the lady's man, but his chubby young roommate was the one with a significant other. Several months after arriving, my uncle Javier fell in love with a Peruvian woman who would visit her sister a few doors down from us on the weekends. I understood. Who could ever turn down eating *lomo saltado* every day? Peruvians didn't invent ceviche (the Inca Empire did, which Ecuador was a part of), but they did create an incredible South American stir-fry. The Peruvian woman my uncle fell in love with happened to be the nanny for the kid of a major Hollywood player. My uncle Javier tried to tell me who it was, but the name didn't ring a bell to me. I asked, "Are you sure you don't mean Sylvester Stallone?" Assured of himself, my uncle said: "No, his name is Oliver Stone." I was not allowed to watch any R-rated films. How was I supposed to know who Oliver Stone was?

One dull weekend, my uncle Javier invited my parents and me to Oliver Stone's house. Oliver and his then-wife were going on a vacation, and the house was free if we wanted to visit. My parents and I definitely wanted to visit. My uncle had been spending a lot of time there with his new Peruvian girlfriend, so I was dying to know how people who worked in Hollywood lived. Plus, I was still hoping my uncle was mistaken and we were really going to Sylvester Stallone's house!

It's hard for me to describe specifically what Oliver Stone's Santa Monica house looked like. At the time, I didn't know phrases like *Spanish colonial* or *California ranch*. All I knew was that Oliver Stone's house was the most stunning home I'd ever seen in my life—it was huge and lavish. I considered my grandfather's home in Guayaquil the nicest house I'd ever seen, but it was modest in comparison to this.

I met Oliver Stone's eight-year-old son Sean, who was three years younger than me. I was a bit standoffish because

I was envious that he had a bigger house than me. But Sean was welcoming and asked if I wanted to play basketball. I said sure, but not before my uncle pulled me aside and asked me to please let him win. I nodded, pretending that I would let him and then proceeded to crush him. We were children, and I had to show Sean who was boss. I whipped Sean's ass so hard at basketball that he complained about me to my uncle's Peruvian girlfriend. After draining all those jump shots, I was not allowed to play basketball with Sean anymore.

I apologized to Sean for whooping his ass at basketball and then we became friends again. He gave me a tour of his house. He showed me the places we could play in and the places children weren't allowed to enter. He walked around with such confidence and privilege, as if he had paid for the entire house himself. On the wall, I noticed that Sean had a framed check for a movie he had recently acted in. It was a paycheck for a film called *Born on the Fourth of July*. I don't remember how much it was for, but anything above 20 bucks in those days was a lot to me. Sean was younger than me and already being paid for his work. For a second there, I could have sworn he was the immigrant and not me.

When everyone finally turned in for the night, I stealthily got out of my assigned bed and started snooping around the house. I didn't want to steal anything; it's just that Sean said there were rooms we were not allowed to go into, so I most definitely had to go into them. One of those rooms appeared to be a closet at first, but was really stairs that led to a hidden office on a lower level. I carefully made my way down the dark steps, turned on the lights, and was confronted by stack after stack of file boxes. I could tell Oliver Stone had a wild and curious imagination because they were all file boxes on the same topic: "JFK." I told myself if he ever found out that I was being nosy in his work space, he would understand. I was sure he would have done the same thing if the tables were turned. What impressed me the most about the room was all the paperwork and VHS tapes with handwritten notes on them spread out everywhere. There seemed to be a method to Oliver's madness. I didn't know who JFK was at the time, so you can imagine how shocked I was to discover the gruesome images inside the JFK boxes. There were several folders labeled "The Doors." I didn't know who The Doors were either but was hypnotized by the pictures of their young and vibrant lead singer, Jim Morrison: a former UCLA student turned rock god. I didn't know who Oliver Stone was, but I respected the amount of notes he took. My fourth-grade teacher had just started to show us how to take notes in class. I did not understand the importance of them until I walked into Oliver Stone's house. I couldn't believe one person could collect so much information on a single topic. I wondered what it might be like to know so much about something, to be so passionate about a subject that you would fill boxes and boxes with information about it. Clearly people loved Oliver's work just from the sheer size of his house. Here was a man responsible for the worlds I was enchanted by on the screen, and all this research seemed to be his foundation. It entered my mind that maybe one day I, too, could do something like this.

I remembered Sean told me the downstairs hidden lab was not his dad's real office. His real work space was outside by the pool. I was also told not to go in the outside office, so of course I went. Immediately I was taken aback by Stone's wooden desk. It was the type of table you would see in films about powerful bankers or oil tycoons. There were once again a lot of files and also some weirdly formatted books (that I would later discover to be screenplays) on his desk. The thing that most grabbed my attention, however, were his war pictures that he hung on the wall and framed on his desk. Oliver Stone had served in the army, and it was inspiring to see the pictures of him and his infantry, as well as a few of the medals he'd won while serving in Vietnam. I was mesmerized by the black-and-white picture of him and his brothers in arms. I wondered how many of those men did not return home from war.

At the end of the weekend, my parents and I drove back home to Duarte from Santa Monica. As I looked out the car window, mansions morphed into large homes, which turned into apartment complexes. American prosperity seemed to decline the farther east we drove on the freeway. I walked inside our apartment and realized that our entire place was nearly the same size as one of Oliver Stone's offices. It would take me years to realize what being exposed to that Santa Monica office did to my young, impressionable mind. That office showed me a world of endless possibilities. A universe of wild curiosity. I was nine years old and there was no way for me to unsee that writer's lab. I may have been living in a small apartment in Duarte at the time, but in my head, I was already living in Oliver Stone's office.

Don't Speak Spanish

In the fall of 1989, my dad lost his job at the sleep center. I'm sure it had to do with his immigration status. With one less household income coming in and the monthly bills demanding to be paid on time, my dad was desperate. That's when he received a call from the Ecuadorian. My dad was surprised to get a call from this man because the last time he saw him, he was being hauled away by the FBI.

My dad had gotten word that a friend of a friend was hiring a full-time medical reports specialist. Since the potential employer was an older Ecuadorian (i.e., "the Ecuadorian"), my dad thought the man would be sympathetic to his situation. My dad lined up an interview for 9 a.m. on a brisk Monday morning. Excited about his new job prospect, he got to the never-before-seen office thirty minutes early. It was pretty far from Duarte and he was a little bit early, so my dad took the opportunity to get gas before the meeting at a station across the street from the office. As he pumped, he looked over at the building where the interview was supposed to take place and saw two federal vans pull up in front of it. Men wearing FBI jackets came running out. Within moments, everyone inside the building, including the older Ecuadorian my dad was supposed to interview with, were escorted into the vans with their hands zip-tied behind their backs. My dad started to shake as he put the gas pump back in its place. He got inside his car and slowly drove away without calling any attention to himself.

Now on the phone with him again, my dad listened as the Ecuadorian claimed it was all one big misunderstanding with the US government, and argued that the proof was in the fact that he was not behind bars. The Ecuadorian offered my dad a great-paying full-time job doing medical reports. The timing was crazy. My dad was skeptical about tossing in his hat with someone who'd had zip ties around his wrists the last time he saw him, but he had been applying everywhere, and nobody else would take a chance on him. Was it his broken English? Was it his lack of immigration papers? Was it a combination of both? My dad knew we couldn't survive simply off my mom's Kmart salary. That's when the Ecuadorian sweetened the pot: "Your wife is a doctor, too, right? I can hire her as a physical therapist for us." Without any good job options as undocumented immigrants, my parents accepted the Ecuadorian's offer. My mom put in her two weeks' notice at Kmart, and we moved to San Clemente, California, which was two hours south. I did not want to go. I cried at the thought of losing all my new American friends.

Part of Marine Corps Base Camp Pendleton is in San Clemente so moving there was frightening for my parents. We were undocumented immigrants purposely moving into a military town, which also had an immigration checkpoint that my parents purposefully avoided. The town was a charming beachside community wrapped in an oversize American flag. San Clemente was very conservative, more conservative than my dad. For the first time since leaving Ecuador, we lived around a lot of people who were white. My parents smiled, were polite, and always kept to themselves. I took all my cues from them. We did not speak unless spoken to.

My grandparents came to visit us in San Clemente. I was ecstatic to finally see them again. This was the longest period I had ever gone without being in their presence. My grandparents arrived at our new apartment and they were delighted for us. They liked our new community and loved that we lived so close to the beach. In Ecuador, we always made a point to go to the beach at least once a month, so this reminded them of home.

One thing that had changed since Ecuador was I noticed that my grandma was squeaking a lot when she walked. It was strange. She did not make any noise while she sat down, but squeaked every time she got up and walked around. Curious, I asked her what that noise was. She put her index finger to her lips, and then revealed that she was wearing Saran Wrap around her belly. It was just one of the many life hacks my grandma taught me: Saran Wrap makes the best girdles. Boy, I had missed her.

My grandparents only stayed with us for the summer. When fall came around, it was time for me to enroll at my new school. I was entering fifth grade. On my first day at Truman Benedict Elementary, my tall blond teacher, Ms. Lovemark, asked me to stand up and spell the word *army* in front of the entire class. Like a true immigrant, I stood and said: "Armí: A-R-M-I. Armí." My new classmates glared at me. *Army*, apparently, was one of the words you were not allowed to misspell in San Clemente. My classmates had been saying the word since birth. Before "mommy" or "daddy" there was "army." The class looked at me for an excruciatingly long moment, and then broke out into laughter.

I sat by myself during recess. I wasn't sure how I was going to fit in at Truman Benedict. I had my cousin Choli in Walnut and my immigrant friends in Duarte—I did not have anybody in San Clemente. This was going to be tricky. At lunch, I spotted some kids from my class playing softball together. I had a good swing, thanks to my cousin Raul, so I figured this would be the perfect way to make some friends. I wrote my name down on the clipboard that hung from the dugout fence. "Rafael" looked so foreign compared to all the Johnnys, Billys, and Nathans on that list. Before I could put down the clipboard, a red dodgeball rolled up to my feet. I looked up and saw Brooke walking toward me. Brooke was a fair-skinned fifth grader with long, flowing brown hair. The brown hair made her stand out in a school predominantly made up of Lannisters.

"Hi," said Brooke gently.

"Umm...I'm signing up for softball," I mumbled.

Brooke smiled and asked, "Can I have my ball back?"

I picked up the red dodgeball and carefully placed it in Brooke's outstretched hands, hoping that the gesture of me simply bending over would blow her away.

"Thanks."

Brooke then looked at the blue Mickey Mouse T-shirt I was wearing.

"That's a cool shirt," quipped Brooke before running back to play with her girlfriends. From that day on, I never took my blue Mickey Mouse T-shirt off.

A few weeks later, due to some miraculous twist of fate, Ms. Lovemark partnered Brooke and me up in class. I couldn't believe it. The prettiest girl in school was now my science assignment partner. I was nervous. All I'd ever said to Brooke up to that point was, "Umm...I'm signing up for softball." I wish I had put some Saran Wrap around my belly to make myself look skinnier. I wish I had combed my hair, or the uni-brow I was rocking at the time. Brooke sat next to me.

"I like your shirt. Mickey's cool."

I nervously smiled to let her know that I was listening.

In an attempt to teach us about how chromosomes worked, Ms. Lovemark walked around the class and handed out white pieces of paper with big circles in the middle of them. She asked the pairs—in this case Brooke and me—to determine which of our physical features our make-believe child (i.e., the circle in the middle of the paper) would inherit. You heard right, Brooke and I were about to have a baby! The exercise consisted of us talking about which were the most common family traits between us, and to come to a consensus on the appearance of our child's face. The problem was that I was too nervous to talk. My parents always seemed uncomfortable around white authority figures, and I had, unfortunately, inherited that trait. I started to perspire. Making babies was making me feel a little nauseous. I had barely started exploring my body at the time. It all seemed so sudden.

Brooke took the initiative and asked me all the questions: "Does your family mostly have brown eyes or blue eyes?" I simply said "yes" or "no" to everything. Brooke had brown hair and I had black hair, so our child's hair would naturally be darker. Brooke had light brown eyes like I did, so we reached for the brown crayons. The more we drew and colored, the more our child was starting to resemble a human being. Brooke wanted a boy, so gosh darn it, we were having a boy. I figured that's the way it worked in real life: women just got what they asked for. Historically, I was ignorantly misinformed. Our boy shared most of Brooke's facial characteristics, which was fine by me. I liked the idea of being able to say, "He takes after his mother." I glanced over at the other drawings in class, each hand-drawn child lighter than the next. Blue eyes and blond hair were the norm for this project. So much so that Ms. Lovemark had to bring out more blue and yellow crayons. Brooke and I were content with our plain old brown crayons.

Sure, our child would be looked at funny, and probably could not spell "army," but it didn't matter. He was ours and we were going to love him unconditionally no matter what he or they looked like. I even made a mental note to teach our child about Peter Pan as soon as humanly possible.

Brooke put down the crayon and proudly held up our new-drawn for the first time. This was not quite the miracle of childbirth I'd been expecting, but it was pretty close. Our boy looked lovely, just like Brooke. I was one proud papa. Who knew I was so good at making babies? I mean, I was Latin American so I had a sneaking suspicion I would be.

"Oh, wait a minute," Brooke said as she dropped our child back on the table and reached for a blue crayon. Now deflated, I looked away. I should have known it was too good to be true. Why wouldn't Brooke want her child to have blue eyes like the rest of the class? Why would she want to have a kid with me anyway? From all the English language media I took in at the time, Brooke seemed way above my evolutionary station. Could I even afford child support? These were real concerns I failed to consider before we started drawing. This is why you should always use protection. Brooke put down the blue crayon and lifted up the drawing once more. I was surprised to see that our son now had a blue Mickey Mouse on his chest.

"Can I keep it?" Brooke asked.

I nodded, delighted that she was happy.

After school that day, I was determined to confess my love for Brooke once and for all. The stars aligned for us to draw a child into existence. I walked to the front of the school where the kids who didn't have to take the bus like I did lined up to wait for their parents. I looked around for Brooke. I finally spotted her flowing brown hair curbside. I swallowed my self-doubt and walked right up to her.

"Hi."

"Oh, hi."

"Umm...we have a son together."

"Yeah, he's very handsome." Brooke pulled out our child from her binder. She asked, "What should we name him?"

"Uh, I don't know." I looked at the school marquee behind me and said, "What about Truman?"

"No, I don't like that name. How about Rafael? That's a pretty name."

I was speechless. Brooke liked my name. She didn't want a Bradley, or Ricky, or Wyatt—she wanted a Rafael! This meant that she saw past my ethnic shortcomings. Was she as in love with me as I was with her? Like a good Latino boy, I was ready to move her and our drawing into my parents' apartment. At that exact moment, a stern voice pierced the air: "Brooke!" Brooke and I turned to see a muscular white man with a marine crew cut. It was Brooke's father. The self-doubt reentered my body. Brooke turned to me and said, "See you tomorrow." She walked over to her dad, gave him a kiss on the cheek, and handed him our new-drawn. She hopped inside his red pickup truck as her dad studied his new grandson. He looked up and squinted his eyes at me. He did not seem to approve of my potential union with his daughter. If "Get off my front lawn" had a face, it was definitely Brooke's dad's. He scrutinized me for a second and then walked around his Dodge Ram, got inside his truck, and drove off with Brooke. That was the first time I remember feeling unworthy of something. In this particular case, it was Brooke's affection.

While I wasn't making many friends at my new school, my parents and I at least became closer. I became the official translator of our household. Any phone calls, teacher conferences, or conversations with the landlord included me as my parents' official English language representative. It must have been demeaning for them to have their ten-year-old translate for them, although we all tried to make the best of an uncomfortable situation. But no translation exchange was more uncomfortable for me than the one with the sleazy door-to-door encyclopedia salesman. Before Wikipedia, there were these things called encyclopedias (or physical wikipedia, if you will), and none was more famous than *Encyclopedia Britannica*. The door-to-door salesman knocked on our apartment one day, and I was asked to translate as he tried to convince my dad to purchase an entire set of encyclopedias—for my sake! In other words, I was translating for this unknown stranger as he tried to ruin my life. Spanish language books in the apartment meant that my mom and dad had to read them, but English language books meant that *I* had to read them. I did not want my dad to buy the *Encyclopedia Britannica*, but I also didn't want to alter my translation of the conversation because I knew I would get in trouble. After an insufferable hour of translating,

my dad finally caved. He bought the complete set of encyclopedias from this man. Dad regretted his decision of paying for
the encyclopedias the moment the door-to-door salesman left
with his money. But as opposed to donating the encyclopedias
to a local school or nonprofit, my dad made himself feel better by forcing me to read them. He decided to make me write
book reports that he claimed he would read after work, but
never did. After several weeks of book reports, I realized they
were going unread, so without my dad's knowledge, I began
recycling them. This was our routine until he finally stopped
asking me for the damn reports. This was how he convinced
himself that he was getting his money's worth. I know a lot
of useless American history because of the *Encyclopedia Britannica*, including the fact that Alexander Hamilton was staunchly
anti-immigrant. Good thing we don't have an entire musical
celebrating his life. Kidding! Lin-Manuel Miranda is a freakin'
genius. How do I know? Because he probably grew up with
the *Encyclopedia Britannica* in his home!

On a warm Sunday morning, my dad decided to take my
mom and me on a stroll to the beach. We lived so close, but
rarely went. We were walking down the sidewalk, enjoying
the waves crashing on the shore, when a man elbowed past
as he ran for his life. He was wearing dirty jeans and a faded
flannel, an outfit typical of the men who worked on the lawns
of the extravagant San Clemente houses near the waterfront.
Two men in official-looking jackets then sprinted past us and
tackled the running man. Confused, I looked up at my dad
and asked, *"Papi, que esta pasando?"* With fear in his eyes,

my dad turned to me and whispered angrily: "Don't speak Spanish!"

I went silent.

The running man did not put up a fight when he was apprehended. He knew his fate, as he was escorted inside the back of a nearby van. I, however, didn't know what would happen to him. But I was too scared to ask after being told not to speak Spanish, especially after my mom explained that we had just witnessed an immigration raid.

When we got home that evening, we did not talk about the beach incident right away. We continued with our day as if nothing unusual had happened. My mom asked me, *"Qué quieres comer?"* I responded, "I don't know, I'll eat whatever." She smiled, and in Spanish said she would make chicken. Later that night I went with my dad to the video store. My dad asked me, *"Qué película quieres ver?"* I replied, "Can we please rent *Terminator 2*?" My dad nodded, and in Spanish said no problem. Later at home, we watched a young John Connor teach the terminator how to say Spanish language phrases like, *"Hasta la vista,* baby." Ironic, since from that day forward and until the middle of high school, I stopped speaking Spanish. My parents would speak to me in Spanish, but I would respond in English. I continued to translate for them, but even that duty died shortly thereafter. When my dad told me to not speak Spanish in front of the immigration officers, I knew he meant for me not to speak Spanish at that moment. At the same time, however, I was so unsettled by the sheer terror in his eyes that I internalized his instruction and refused to speak Spanish to anybody—even my family—for many years. This was a man I had seen save a child's life. He was the closest thing to a superhero I had ever known. For something to cause him that much dread was enough for me to reconsider how I interacted with the world. After that beach incident, I did not feel it was safe to continue speaking Spanish.

Alien Life Form

My parents worked Monday through Friday, with no time off for federal holidays. If I did not have school on a given day, I would have to accompany my mom to work. She would do physical therapy with her patients while I watched TV in the employee break room. Before streaming or premium cable, daytime network programming during the week was terrible. I would surf through five broadcast channels and a lot of court shows before I found one station that at least had reruns. When I first saw Ricky Ricardo in *I Love Lucy*, it blew my mind. Ricky's angry Spanish rants sounded just like my dad's! I had no idea American households sounded like mine. It was, like, *Oh, Latinos have been in this country all along.* Of course, the heartbreaking thing was that *I Love Lucy* was it for the Latino community in Hollywood for quite some time.

The Ecuadorian who ran the medical reports company that employed my parents made a pact with my dad that he would not take part in any shady business deals as long as my parents were working for him. But it was only a matter of time before he reverted to his old ways. No matter how much my dad tried to convince himself otherwise, the FBI raided the Ecuadorian's business the first time around for a reason. Reviewing some medical reports one morning, my dad noticed his boss was committing insurance fraud. My dad confronted the old man, and he was surprised when the Ecuadorian threatened him and my mom with their immigration status. The whole time they worked for him, he never brought up the fact that they were undocumented—he had kept that card close to his vest. Now they realized that the Ecuadorian had planned to use this leverage on them all along. The tension between my parents and the three other family members the Ecuadorian employed kept building at the office, until it came to a boiling point. The Ecuadorian started screaming at my mom one day for no apparent reason. My mom had never been screamed at by a man in her life, except for maybe my grandfather, of course, so she was frozen in shock. Hearing all the commotion, my dad ran down the stairs, shoved the old man against the wall, and threatened to kick his ass if he ever screamed at his wife again. The Ecuadorian fired my parents on the spot. It did not matter because they had already decided that they had to leave anyway. The Ecuadorian was raided by the FBI again later that same year. My parents, of course, kept all of this from me, which allowed me to have a completely different experience from theirs. One that was annoying because of the constant moving, as opposed to being crippled by the fear of almost being apprehended by the federal government.

My dad lived by the motto that you always had to keep two jobs while in this country, so by the time he left the medical reports industry, he had already begun working in magnetic resonance imaging (MRI). He found a joyous Chinese businessman that was impressed by the fact that my dad was a doctor in a foreign country. The Chinese man was a doctor himself, and went by the awe-inspiring name of Dr. Ninja. It was rumored that Dr. Ninja was trained in the dark martial arts of ninjutsu. It might have been a rumor that he himself had started since the license plate on his new Ferrari stated: DR NINJA. Also, let's not hang a lantern on the fact that ninjas were Japanese and that this man was Chinese. What mattered was that Dr. Ninja was a fellow immigrant and that he gave my dad his first job in MRI.

When the Ecuadorian fired my parents, my dad turned to Dr. Ninja and asked if he had any full-time positions for him and his wife. Dr. Ninja's MRI business was growing in Thousand Oaks, California, so he agreed to hire my dad full-time. Plus, his medical center was also in need of a new physical therapist. My mom was a perfect candidate. On top of everything, Dr. Ninja also had an available two-bedroom unit at an apartment complex he owned. It made perfect sense for him to give my parents full-time employment so they could then turn around and use their salaries to pay him rent. The deal was made and we moved to Thousand Oaks.

Thousand Oaks was in Ventura County, which was located neatly between Santa Barbara and Los Angeles. Driving around Thousand Oaks, I noticed that it was whiter than

San Clemente, if that was even possible. That made me feel slightly uncomfortable. It was truly a beautiful place to live, unless, of course, you valued diversity. When I'd wondered what America would be like as a child in Ecuador, this conservative city was exactly what I'd imagined. I would be remiss not to mention that Thousand Oaks was one of the many cities in California that was founded on white flight (the phenomena that occurred when white folks took their wealth out of metropolitan cities when too many Black residents and other minorities moved in) and redlining (Federal Housing Administration policies that encouraged real estate interests to concentrate people of color away from white homeowners). On top of that town history, my parents and I landed there to remind them that they could not escape us no matter how hard they tried.

Aspen Elementary was fantastic. It was a well-funded school with really attentive teachers. The biggest surprise came on my first day when two of my new classmates asked me where I was from. It must have been my wardrobe that had tipped them off, because I had pretty much gotten rid of my accent in San Clemente. I replied that I was from Ecuador. One of the girls immediately got excited.

"I've been there. I went to Quito and Guayaquil with my parents two years ago. It's beautiful."

This was the first time I had ever met anybody at a public school who knew where Ecuador was, let alone had visited it, who wasn't my cousin. Most students in Southern California just assumed Ecuador was a state in Mexico. That was how

I knew I was dealing with different kinds of white people in Thousand Oaks. These school students were cultured and well traveled. They were not just white people. They were rich white people.

I joined the local soccer league and was happy to discover that some of my classmates were also on the team I was assigned to. We all became friends, and our friendship spilled into the classroom. One of the kids was Nate, a short white kid with glasses and red hair who looked like the prototype for Dexter on *Dexter's Laboratory*. I liked Nate, but he would always make comments about the kind of car my mom drove, which was nowhere near as fancy as his mom's Lexus. Whatever, I had kids to hang out with at school for the first time in a long time, and that was all that mattered. Subsequently, I started thriving as a student. I was happy. It had only been a few months, but Aspen Elementary was already the best experience I'd had in school.

After soccer practice one evening, I jumped in the car and asked my mom if we could go to McDonald's. My mom told me we could, but that first she wanted to tell me something.

"We have to move again," she said apologetically.

"But we just got here," I pleaded, hoping that my whine would change her mind.

"I'm sorry, sweetie. We have to. Your dad and I lost our jobs."

I was disappointed. My poor mom felt terrible, but what could she do? Being immigrants in this country was not easy, and good-paying jobs were very hard to come by for them.

I, on the other hand, hated not being able to make any real friends wherever we went. That night as we were having dinner, I noticed that my dad did not want to speak about anything. Just from his brooding alone, I knew it was time to pack my bags.

On one of my last days at Aspen Elementary, only three months in, we were all asked to join a school assembly. We sat on the floor as the principal went over important announcements. Information I assumed didn't matter to me because I would be leaving. One of those announcements was for Student of the Month. The principal shockingly stated, "We are proud to announce that the first Student of the Month award goes to...Rafael."

I was surprised to hear my name. A little startled, really. It had been a long time since I had been recognized for anything. In Ecuador, I was always asked to give speeches as the head of my class. But the same was not true in the United States. I'd felt like I was slipping between the cracks in all my previous schools. First it was my lack of English, then it was my lack of friends, but ultimately, it was my lack of stability. We moved so much that I couldn't catch up in most learning environments. I was always the new kid in the corner who went unnoticed. It was hard to be engaged. I did pretty well with my grades throughout, but in Thousand Oaks I really hit my stride. I was noticed, I made friends, and my teachers were attentive. Well-funded schools just hit different.

The students all clapped for me. I walked to the front,

grabbed my certificate, looked out at the audience, and was surprised to see my mom and dad. Apparently the school had called them to let them know I was receiving the award so they could be in attendance. After the ceremony, I ran up to my parents, happy to see them. Nate, my white friend from soccer, walked by and said, "You only won that 'cause you're leaving." I was taken aback by Nate's comment. He might have been right. This all could have been Aspen Elementary's very thoughtful good-bye present to me, but why did Nate feel the need to point that out? It was not the possible truth of what Nate said that bothered me. It was the sense of entitlement with which he'd said it, almost as if he was certain that the award was his if not for my leaving. Maybe I did not deserve the Student of the Month award, but why would Nate simply assume it was his to begin with?

With no jobs, my parents had no choice but to take up an old friend's offer to move in with him and his family. I could tell this was hard on them. They looked wearier than in past moves. Like my parents, the Espinozas were also doctors from Ecuador, which was where they had met originally, so going from being medical professionals in South America to taking any job just to survive in the United States was something they understood. Of course, the Espinozas had three children—all around my age. As previously at my aunt Teresa's house, I was allowed to sleep inside the house with the kids. My parents, however, supported monetarily in the construction of an attached room to the house, which they then lived in. The

Espinozas did not ask my parents for any rent money. All my parents had to do was buy all the food for the household. It seemed like a great offer to two immigrants without work.

Panorama City was not like Thousand Oaks. The streets were not as clean. There was more delinquency. Parents did not feel safe letting their children outside of the house after a certain time. There was more smog than Thousand Oaks, and there was a lot more noise pollution. It was like night and day for me.

I was still slightly down because of the move. In the past, we would move into another apartment building, but this time around we had to move in with another family. A family that I barely knew. On our first Saturday with the Espinozas, in an attempt to cheer me up, my mom surprised me by saying: "Put on your soccer clothes—we're going to your game!"

I was elated. I had given up on the idea of attending any more soccer games. Thousand Oaks was so far away that I figured we would never return. I quickly put on my shorts and soccer cleats and jumped inside my mom's car. We hit the road. We drove an hour and a half in traffic from Panorama City to Ventura County, singing Paula Abdul all the way there. When we got to the field, we were stunned to discover that it was completely empty.

"What's going on?" wondered my mom.

One of the field workers approached the car and told us that we had missed the game by four hours. My mom looked at her calendar defeated, feeling like she couldn't even do this one thing right.

"Don't worry, Mom," I said. "Let's just go to McDonald's and crank up the Paula Abdul."

My mom smiled and the two of us hit the road again. I missed an awful lot of soccer games that year, but I didn't care because I got to spend most of the weekends in the car with my best friend singing "Straight up now tell me."

Picking up where I left off in sixth grade, I was enrolled in Panorama City Elementary with my three new roommates: Andres, Paco, and David. We all liked each other, but I always felt like the odd man out, given their tight brotherly love. The teachers and staff at Panorama City Elementary were nice, but they all seemed overworked. Classrooms were too full and there didn't seem to be enough counselors for the students. My new teacher was a balding white male with bifocals who still looked to be in great shape. There was a big, intimidating kid in class who stood out. Andres, who was in the same class as me, and I never spoke to him. In fact, all the kids in class avoided ever making eye contact with him in fear they might set him off. One tense morning, when the teacher had us each read out loud from our textbooks, the intimidating kid refused to do so. The teacher pushed back, triggering the kid to throw a tantrum. He stood and flipped his desk in defiance. He screamed profanities at the teacher and started flailing his arms wildly. It was abundantly clear that I was not in Thousand Oaks anymore. The teacher rushed over and physically restrained the poor kid, who was clearly pleading for help. But nobody would help him—teachers would just restrain him. It was a terrible situation all around.

At least recess and lunch were fun. Andres, Paco, David, and I would meet up on the jungle gym to play. Everything was going well until we heard loud gunshots go off on the playground. The principal shouted for us to duck and get down on the ground. We all did as we were told. After a few moments, it was evident that the gunshots were not aimed at the school. There were immediate debates as to whether they were gunshots at all. In any case, we were allowed to stand and go back to playing. Sadly, the bell rang and recess was over.

When I was home alone, I would watch a lot of American television to pass the time. I discovered a show called *Full House*, which didn't seem that full compared to our current living situation. There was also a show called *Family Matters*, where the main character was a minority teenager who was nerdier than I was, which instantly made me feel better about myself. And then there was *ALF*. A high-concept family sitcom about a puppet alien living with a suburban middle-class family (the Tanners). *ALF* stood for "Alien Life Form." I loved all things puppet-related back then. So between my affinity for puppets and my love of American TV, *ALF* was the perfect show for me. In one episode, ALF tried to convince the president of the United States to slow down the American nuclear program or suffer the same fate as his home planet of Melmac, which exploded after everyone plugged in their hair dryer at the same time. That was the kind of good family fun you would expect tuning into *ALF*.

One ordinary evening, I was calmly watching a new episode of *ALF* when the Tanners suddenly got a phone call from the government saying that they knew they were harboring an alien. The entire family freaked out, as did I! None of us wanted ALF to be captured by the government's Alien Task Force. The Tanners tried to hide ALF the best they could, but it was to no avail. The government descended on the Tanners' home and said they knew they were harboring an alien...an *illegal* alien. The laugh track kicked in. The government was in search of illegal aliens, not aliens from outer space. This was all one big misunderstanding. The government was conducting a routine immigration raid and ALF ultimately had nothing to worry about. The federal agents left and ALF came out from hiding. The Tanners and ALF laughed out loud as the show faded to black with the audience applause.

April 29, 1992

My parents were both able to find full-time employment, which meant we could afford to get our own apartment once more. We said good-bye to the Espinozas and Panorama City, packed our cars, and headed to Monrovia, California, where I was to start middle school. Between the extremes of Thousand Oaks and Panorama City, I felt ready for whatever Monrovia public schools would throw at me.

Santa Fe Middle School was not as bad as I'd feared. Yes, there were some kids who were developing faster than others. There was a lot of sex being talked about in the bathrooms, and some boys even pulled out their penises in the back of the class so that the giggling curious girls could touch them. But despite that, the majority of us were just dorks at heart. We simply wanted to play basketball. The big problem was that I wasn't good at basketball. I peaked when I kicked Oliver Stone's son's ass, and it was all downhill after that.

It was 1992. The era of Michael Jordan and Scottie Pippen.

A lot of kids in our LA County middle school were wearing Chicago Bulls gear. That felt blasphemous to me. I was a hardcore Lakers fan. Well, more specifically, a Magic Johnson fan. When my grandfather came to stay with us in San Clemente, we would watch a lot of basketball games together. It was how my dad, grandpa, and I bonded. My grandfather's nickname in Ecuador was El Negro (i.e., "the Black Man"), but my grandfather did not like Black people. I'll give you a second to digest that. A darker-skinned Ecuadorian who was called "the Black Man" but did not like Black people. My grandfather was filled with a lot of self-hate that could fill an entire book. But I mention it because I want you to understand how impacted I was when he said during a live Lakers game:

"I love Magic Johnson."

I was speechless. I was more stunned by my grandfather's comment than I was of Magic's no-look pass on live television. Magic Johnson changed my grandfather's view of Black athletes, and subsequently of other Black people. He no longer criticized them or made backhanded remarks when he saw them on TV. He proudly cheered them on as the Lakers played, and it took the greatest point guard ever to play the game to accomplish that.

All the cool kids at school played basketball, so if I was going to fit in, in seventh grade, I would have to learn to play the game, and play it well. Fortunately, our new apartment complex had a basketball hoop in the parking lot, which could be accessed once there were no cars parked under it. I shot hoops every day from the time I got home from school until the first car parked under the basket. I put in the work, I was highly dedicated, but I was still terrible. I didn't have anybody to show me the proper shot form. My dad was good at basketball, but he got a new job at a vocational school teaching previously incarcerated individuals how to work as surgical assistants, so he was gone all the time. He caught me shooting hoops once, grabbed my rebound, sank a three-pointer, and then left for work without teaching me how he did it.

I nervously stood by the court at lunch the next day waiting to be picked on a team. I really wanted to be wanted, but nobody picked me. I was afraid I would go friendless at this school. That's when Rodney, a charismatic Black kid with a million-dollar smile whom everyone wanted to be friends with, and who also happened to be the best player on the court, decided to take a chance on me.

"I'll take Rafael," said Rodney. "Why not?"

Rodney was so good, he knew he could win with me as a disadvantage. The game started and I stayed in the back court. The ball got stripped out of Rodney's hands by the opposing team. They were on a fast break down the court and would have made it, if not for me being there to block the shot. I was big for my age, so I was an imposing defender just by standing there. Rodney ran back, grabbed the rebound, and tossed it to the other end of the court, where a teammate made an easy layup. Rodney turned to me and said, "Good job." I smiled, not realizing how clever my choice to focus on defense was. No kid ever wanted to play defense because everyone just wanted to show off on the offense. I exclusively began playing defense, and Rodney continued to pick me on his team. As a result, everyone started accepting me at school simply because I was one of Rodney's boys.

Walking home from school one day, I discovered that Rodney lived in the apartment building behind mine, so we walked home together. We started to hang out more. Rodney would come over to our apartment and we would do homework together, we would watch TV together, we would even listen to the new Boyz II Men and Kris Kross albums together. It was safe to say that Rodney and I were friends. Then April 29, 1992, happened. We were told to stay home from school as we watched Los Angeles burn in the news. My mom and I were glued to the TV. She called my uncle Ivan to make sure he was safe after seeing his work building up in flames. Time and time again, the news referred to what was happening as "a riot." I was eleven years old and nothing that I saw on TV made any sense to me.

When we eventually went back to school, Rodney was a little distant. He was still nice to me because that was his nature, but there seemed to be some kind of new invisible barrier between us. "Hey," I would wave. Rodney would nod his head and keep walking. Nobody played basketball at lunch for a week.

Rodney eventually stopped walking home with me after school. Instead, he preferred to hang out with other Black kids. He stopped coming over to our apartment altogether. I tried so hard to get Rodney to like me initially that when he actually did, I thought nothing could ever break that bond. I wasn't ready for race to be a topic in our friendship, or in my life in general. A lot of us were privileged enough not to think about race if we didn't want to. American students like Rodney, however, had no choice but to deal with it every day—simply due to the color of their skin. From all the previous schools I had attended in Southern California, I knew that I was not white. But after April 29, 1992, I also discovered that I was not Black. Unfortunately, the concept of race in America is mostly understood as a black and white paradigm. Anything outside of that dichotomy gets ignored. I did not know where I, as a young Latino, fit in, in all of this. Our school system did a poor job talking about race. No teacher at school brought up what had happened after the Rodney King verdict. We all saw what happened on TV, but nobody talked about it. A few students bragged about how they knew people who were "down there jacking stuff." As immigrants, my parents were just shocked that things could get so violent on the streets of America. They had left the political turmoil of South America in part for that reason.

I was an immigrant kid yearning for his friend. I did not understand the generational trauma that Rodney must have been going through. I did not understand why Black people took to the streets to begin with, the history of policing in communities of color, or what the murder of the young Latasha Harlins before the verdict that acquitted the LAPD officers who had clearly used excessive force against an unarmed Rodney King had to do with any of it. I wanted my friend back, but all I got in return was a lot of racial tension that continued to go unaddressed. Rodney and I stopped hanging out. He stuck more with the Black kids, and I in turn had no choice but to stick with the Latino kids. We all further segregated ourselves.

At this time, my dad was working a full-time job in East LA with people who had previously had a difficult time with the criminal justice system and wanted to turn their lives around. He was working at a vocational school teaching nontraditional students to become surgical assistants. The job was great for my dad, who loved to pretend he was still the head surgeon in his mock emergency rooms. The problem was that my dad had a thick accent, and these first-generation ex-gangbangers were not having it. They were quite infuriated that my dad did not speak perfect English. It affected their learning, which in turn affected their future prospects. There was clearly a communication breakdown between both parties.

One tense day in class, during an excruciatingly long technical lecture that even my dad hated giving, the MCIC (main chola in charge) shouted: "Stop talking!" My dad froze. He didn't know what to do. Also, no one ever yells at the head surgeon—they are the ones who do all the yelling. The MCIC continued: "These lectures are a joke. We can't even understand you!" Concerned that his students might get violent, my dad asked in his broken English, "What do you suggest we should do?" The MCIC stood up, walked to the front of the class, and got up in my dad's face. Now nose to nose, my dad knew too well this battle-hardened woman from the streets could cause him great physical harm. The MCIC looked my short, skinny dad up and down. "We'll make you a deal. You teach us how to work in the ER, and we'll teach you English. Deal?" "Deal," said my dad, letting out a sigh of relief, not knowing this would be the best deal he would ever receive in this country.

As the months passed, my dad got in sync with his tough, ex-gang-banging students. He even learned how to say, "'Sup," without looking like a dork. My dad got better and better at speaking English thanks to them, which in turn made it a lot easier for them to learn. The MCIC was eight-and-a-half-months pregnant by this point. She was huge. One bitter day, my dad got home incredibly late from work. When my mom asked where he'd been, he told her the most remarkable story ever. This is the one story I cannot verify, but think it is important to share.

My dad claimed that he was teaching the difference between a surgical scalpel and a needle driver when the MCIC's water broke in the middle of class. She went straight into labor and nothing was going to stop that baby from entering the world. My dad ran over to the MCIC to make sure she was okay, and right as he commanded for somebody to call an ambulance, she made one simple request of him: "I want you to deliver my baby." Without taking a second to consider, my dad turned the entire class into a makeshift operating room. Everybody got around him and they each put into practice what they had been learning all those past months. The MCIC screamed, which attracted outside attention to the class. A short cholo quickly locked the door to prevent anybody from entering.

My dad was helping the MCIC push while the short cholo told the people outside the door to please call an ambulance. When it was all said and done, my dad delivered a healthy seven-and-a-half-pound baby boy—one with no police record and full of potential. The MCIC took the newborn into her loving arms and thanked my dad, who then climbed out the window so that he wouldn't get fired for practicing medicine illegally. My mom and I were made speechless by this story.

My dad got a reputation for being "down," which meant being cool in street slang—one with the pack. My dad started hanging out with his students outside of class a lot. He never took my mom or me near his vocational students, so we never knew what he was up to. Then one day he came home pale in the face. He was fired from his vocational teaching job. My mom and I were shocked. He told us that he gave a sick janitor an antiviral injection, and that the school administration used that as grounds for him having practiced medicine illegally. Since he was not a doctor in this country, my dad said he was fired on the spot. It was yet another remarkable story. I looked up at my mom to see if she believed him. She did. This time my parents did not have to say anything. My dad losing his job meant that we were moving again.

Nuthin' but a G Thang

We moved to West Covina to be closer to our family. For the first time ever, I was excited by a move because West Covina meant that I could be near Choli again. He and I picked up right where we'd left off. We were thick as thieves. But growing up on the West Covina–La Puente border, Choli and I were surrounded by a lot of gang activity. We never joined any gangs—our moms kept too close an eye on us to do such a thing. But Choli and I needed to be tough around our neighborhood. Teenagers suffering from toxic masculinity and economic inequality can always smell fear, so my cousin and I had to be fearless.

Fun fact, Choli and I fought each other only once in our lives. It was the Great Tom Hanks–Will Smith War of '91. The battle was over what TV show to watch in his house. I should have known how passionate I would become about episodic storytelling as an adult because Choli wanted to watch *The Fresh Prince of Bel-Air* and I was ready to get into a fistfight to

watch reruns of *Bosom Buddies*. Can you imagine? A fat Hispanic kid fighting for the honor of Tom Hanks in drag! We
first fought over the remote control. Then fists started flying. Screams were let out. In the end, Choli pinned me to the
ground, which meant he was the victor. Except that he was
crying and I was not, so in our tough little neighborhood that
meant it was a tie.

On one of the first weekends I moved in, Choli and I
walked over to Nogales High School. We were both about
to start Rincon Intermediate, which was a feeder school to
Nogales High that had a reputation of being full of gang activity at the time. Choli and I simply wanted to play handball,
and Nogales High was the only place that had handball courts.
Handball was a very democratic sport. You did not need any
of the expensive equipment and lush fields that baseball and
football required. All you needed was one little blue handball.
There's a reason so many incarcerated and formerly incarcerated individuals play the sport to this day. And if you do not
think handball is a sport, then neither is golf!

Choli and I got in less than one round of handball before
a white male, who looked approximately thirty years of age,
approached us with a gun in his hand. Immediately frightened, my cousin and I dropped the handball on the floor. We
did not know what was happening. Was this one of the gangsters we were warned about at Nogales? The man identified
himself as an undercover cop and accused us of being there
to rob the school. Perplexed, Choli and I disagreed. We were

simply there to play handball. The undercover officer did not believe us. Lying or not, we were only thirteen years old.

The officer locked Choli and me in a dark storage room adjacent to the handball courts while he looked around the premises for the accomplices he insisted we had. We were frightened. We had no idea why he did not believe us. We were certain that once he saw the blue handball, he would let us go. After what felt like an eternity in the darkness, we were finally let out of the tiny room, only to be placed in the back of a squad car. Two additional white police officers had shown up at this point, and the three men looked around the school in search of our imaginary accomplices while we were locked up in the backseat. Mortified, I started to feel like we *had* done something wrong. I mean, why else spend this much energy on two kids unless they had committed some kind of crime? A police car, an undercover cop, two officers on patrol, and three loaded firearms ready to scream—all there to stop two kids from playing handball. We were let go after they could not prove their theory. No apology. They simply opened the squad car door and told us not to come back during nonschool hours.

Choli and I started eighth grade at Rincon. The kids there were tougher than any I had ever encountered. A lot of them were gangbangers or affiliated with gangs. Choli and I didn't belong to any crews, but we were accepted at school simply for being tough, keeping to ourselves, always being respectful, and never ever ratting anyone out. The little gangsters felt safe around Choli and me. So much so that one of them,

Richard, the most intimidating cholo at school, crept up to me one morning and asked: "Do you wanna buy a shotgun?" Richard was not kidding. The guys from his crew had an extra one and he needed to sell it quickly. I thought about buying it for a split second. For as tough as I acted, I always feared I was one confrontation away from serious harm. Maybe I would be safer with a shotgun. Maybe the shotgun would earn me more respect. But then I thought, *Does a thirteen-year-old really need a shotgun?* I also remembered that I didn't have money to buy a shotgun, and had nowhere to hide said shotgun from my parents if I was stupid enough to do so. I told Richard that I was cool, he shrugged, and he continued his discounted sales pitch with another student.

At Rincon Intermediate, we were being forced to grow up faster than more affluent kids our age do. Despite it all, there were a lot of laughs, flirting, and hanging out at the school. My first slow dance was at Rincon, so was my first quinceañera court, for my Salvadorian American friend Nelda. Rincon was not miserable by any stretch of the imagination. But we were always on edge.

It was at this point in our lives, with my dad desperate to find more work, that he received something unexpected in the mail. It was an official letter from an unknown American gentleman who must have had a premonition that my dad was going through a hard time. This stranger's name sounded very rich. It was Ed McMahon, and he had just notified my dad that he may have just won one million dollars. My dad was beside himself. He could not believe his good fortune. It was as if

God was giving him a break for once in his life. One million dollars. There was so much my dad could do with one million dollars. Pay off all the debt he owed. Buy his two cars outright. My dad did not know what to do with all of his excitement. He did not tell my mom or me anything. He hid that official communication from Ed McMahon under his mattress. On the weekend, my uncle Javier came to visit. That's when my dad took him upstairs to his room and shut the door behind them. He told my uncle that he was going to tell him something he had not shared with a single soul. My dad pulled out the letter from under his mattress and said, "I may just have won one million dollars."

My uncle Javier took a second to compose himself, trying to hold it together, but then he erupted into laughter. "You didn't win shit," said my uncle. "That's marketing to get you to buy useless electronics." My dad felt so ashamed that he did not mention the microwave he had already ordered to be eligible for the one million dollars.

I was just as naive as my dad at the time. Walking home from Rincon one day, I noticed that my neighbor Edgar, who was ten years older than me, was playing mariachi on his front patio. I had only heard mariachi music at the Ecuadorian parties that my grandfather used to throw, so up to that point, I had assumed mariachis were from Ecuador. I locked eyes with Edgar and naively asked, "Oh, you listen to Ecuadorian mariachis, too?"

"What the hell are you talking about?" replied Edgar. "Mariachis are from Mexico!"

I did not know.

Despite that rocky start, Edgar and I became fast friends. My parents did not say anything about the fact that I was thirteen hanging out with a twenty-three-year-old. They were just happy I had a new friend after moving me out of my old neighborhood. Edgar was a brawny Mexican American who loved to talk about his past high school football glory. He was essentially a younger, shorter, and browner version of Al Bundy. Edgar was a quintessential guy from the 'hood: tough on the outside, but really a kindhearted kid on the inside. Edgar and I bonded over our love for Vicente Fernandez and comic books. Comics, by the way, were not something I could ever talk about at Rincon, or my cholo friends would clown on me. I knew of the classic DC superhero characters like Batman, Superman, and Wonder Woman from my childhood in Ecuador, but Edgar introduced me to the more "sciency" characters of Marvel. The Hulk and his gamma rays. The radioactive Spider-Man. The tight-knit family of scientists known as the Fantastic Four. And the most important of all to me, the children of the atom: the X-Men. Patterned after Martin Luther King Jr. and Malcolm X, Charles Xavier and Magneto were the perfect models for helping non-Black kids understand the Civil Rights Movement. Anybody who felt different or rejected by society could easily relate to being a mutant. I sure as hell did. I fell in love with the character of Wolverine, a short superhero with a hairy chest, a huge ego, and an attitude problem. Without a doubt, Wolverine was the most Latino superhero I had ever read about! Wolverine also had a drinking problem.

Something I started developing at the time, as Choli and I insisted on drinking alcohol at every family function together.

My everyday uniform was a black bomber jacket and a black White Sox baseball hat. Dr. Dre had dropped *The Chronic* a year earlier and only a pioneer of gangsta rap could get me to turn my back on the Los Angeles Dodgers. He was from Compton, after all, and Compton was now full of immigrants. Dr. Dre knew what was up. I made friends with all the local gangs at school and I even had a girlfriend, or at least I had a girl who said she was my girlfriend and I went along with it. Her name was Jenny. She was sweet and bubbly. A Latina cheerleader in a school where boys were too cool to play sports. We never saw each other outside of class. Her parents were too strict. Jenny and I talked on the phone from time to time. One day after school, Jenny guided me behind the English building and kissed me. But this was no innocent elementary school peck on the lips. This was the French way of showing affection. It was exciting. Jenny's kiss teleported me all the way back to the court of Louis XIV. After that kiss, I was ready for cigarettes, baguettes, and red wine. Jenny and I broke up shortly after that, but that kiss was the most memorable moment of my entire middle school experience. In the immortal words of Snoop Dogg: It was "realer than Real Deal Holyfield."

A Dog Named Monsieur

On July 23, 1993, my mom came home from work early with tears in her eyes. She had been crying in a corner on the floor of the hospital for some time before her employer finally told her to please go home. With her eyes welled up, my mom gently said, "Tata has died." My Tata, the first male figure I ever had in my life, was no longer with us. My mom sobbed in my arms after she told me the terrible news. I was in shock. It was the first major death I had experienced as a kid. It was a lot to process. Plus, I had been secretly suffering from anxiety attacks at the time. I pondered death an awful lot. Perhaps it was because I was an only child and had a lot of free time on my hands. I was overthinking eternity and then freaking myself out pondering the idea of nonexistence. I now realize I was dealing with a death anxiety. The idea of knowing that one day I would no longer be on this earth—that I no longer would have my family around me—was a lot for my young mind to grasp. It kept me up at night. In that vulnerable moment between being awake and asleep, I frightened myself by pondering what nonbeing would feel like. My grandfather's passing forced me to zero in on this anxiety.

The shock of losing my grandfather was nothing compared to what my mom was going through. My mom always saw the positive side of things. When the car broke down, she thought it was great that we got to walk and burn off the big lunch we just had. If we were low on money for groceries, she took it as a fun challenge to make a feast with what little ingredients we had left in the fridge. But the death of her father caused this joyful woman's flame to dim. I had never seen my mom like this. Death is natural. It is part of our human existence. As a doctor, my mom knows this all too well. But experiencing a death while not being able to leave the country to go bury your loved one was something entirely different. My mom was hurting, and the only thing that could give her peace at that moment was to go back to Ecuador to bury her father. But alas, she told me she could not go. This was the exact moment I realized, there's no going back.

When I was younger, my parents breezed over explaining why we couldn't leave the country. I just figured some people could leave and others couldn't. We simply couldn't. Plus, we never really wanted to leave. America was our home. Then my grandfather died. Realizing that we couldn't leave the country at that moment hit me like a sledgehammer to the stomach. Remember, I was anxious about dying at the time. Immigration problems felt minuscule compared to the stress of not being, so I didn't focus on what it meant that we couldn't go back! Not being able to leave the country was just a fact of life that I had accepted without asking as a child. Besides, we moved around California an awful lot. I was tired of traveling. I had gone to seven different elementary schools and middle schools before I got to high school. I had no idea why we moved so much—I figured that was just an American way of life. In my eyes, my parents were like indoor campesinos who followed the work. We lived near the beaches of Orange County as well as the inner cities of Los Angeles County. We lived in Walnut, Duarte, San Clemente, Thousand Oaks, Panorama City, Monrovia, and West Covina. I played for the La Puente Warriors and volunteered at the Huntington Memorial Hospital in Pasadena. We never set down roots anywhere and this was something I got accustomed to. I kept up the practice in my adult life. In fact, after high school I lived in Westwood, Alhambra, Monterey Park, Silver Lake, and Altadena. I'm most likely moving as you read this chapter.

It was quite frustrating to learn that we could move freely throughout California but were not allowed to travel internationally. No matter how badly she wanted to accompany all her siblings back to Guayaquil, my mom was not allowed to return to Ecuador. For the first time ever, I wondered if my mom considered going back for good. I wondered if losing her father made her question what this American experiment was all for. At the end of the day, my mom most cherished being around her family. Not being able to leave the country because she would then not be allowed back in was heart-wrenching for her. She later told me she spent the night wondering if there was anything she could do. Was there any way to go and support her mother, bury her father, and then come back? There wasn't. The immigration problems my mom found herself in did not care about the loss of life. They did not care about a death in the family. Through her pain, my mom knew there was nothing that could be done. This was the life she chose. This was the life she chose for her son. Now as an adult, it's hard knowing that she was going through this great pain without my support. There was so much I didn't know then simply because she wanted to protect me.

The very next day, my grandfather had a big funeral. He had requested dueling guitars to be played as he was laid to rest. He also insisted that guests be served Scotch, the same whiskey that took his life prematurely. My grandfather was always larger than life, which was why he died on July 23 and was buried on July 24, the same weekend Guayaquil celebrated its founding 455 years earlier. The local newspaper pointed out that while the city of Guayaquil celebrated, an unlucky few mourned. It stated: *"Si, para la mayoria estuvo presente Guayaquil de mis Amores...Para otros, acaso, hubo un Guayaquil de mis Dolores."* To translate that in English would be to bastardize the writer's poetry. The newspaper writer, by the way, an old friend of my grandfather's, even referred to him as "El Negro Arrata" in publication.

The days went by and nothing my dad and I did would make my mom feel better. Her inner fire was still dim. Then one evening, desperate, my dad asked my mom and me to get in the car. We started driving east to Riverside, I discovered, and we ended up at a dog kennel. My mom instantly brightened up. We were going to get a dog. Our first dog as a family. My mom looked at the litter of cute German shepherds. One hobbled toward my mom. Her motherly, nurturing instinct kicked in as soon as she saw the crippled canine. "That one," she said enthusiastically. Not allowing her to have her moment, my dad whispered, "No, we're paying a lot of money for this dog. Pick a good one." *Fine*, she thought. My mom then made eye contact with Monsieur, which was the very pretentious French name my dad gave my mom's new German shepherd.

My mom loved Monsieur from the moment she laid eyes on him. The two became instant friends. My dad was right. A puppy brought new life to our household. Now mind you that we lived in a condominium with no backyard. Having a German shepherd inside a carpeted house was not a good idea. What's more, I didn't ask for the dog but was expected to take care of it. I was in charge of washing it, feeding it, walking it, and picking up after him. I understand why I would do all this if I had asked for the damn dog. I didn't. And I would have resented this dog if not for seeing how happy he made my mom.

Monsieur and I were cordial. I don't want to mislead you and pretend that we were close. We weren't. Our next dog, Sasha, my mom's black Labrador that she named after her favorite African American coworker (don't worry we had a long conversation about covert racism immediately after the naming), and I were very close. But not Monsieur. Monsieur and I respected each other. I would feed him and walk him accordingly as long as he didn't shit on the carpet. That was the deal. I deeply hated dog shit, so it was important that we each kept our end of the bargain.

It was on one of those long walks with Monsieur around the neighborhood that I realized that I was no longer scared of death. I had been very anxious about dying at such a young age, but that's because I never knew anybody who had gone through it. Now my grandfather was dead. And I felt that if he was brave enough to face his own mortality, then so could I. It's ironic that it took the first father figure of my life to die for me to overcome my fear of death. My fear of dog shit, however, lived on for quite some time.

Under the Table

After Choli and I graduated from Rincon Intermediate, we enrolled in West Covina High School together. We were supposed to go to Nogales High, but our parents were afraid we would turn into gangbangers, so we used friends' addresses and went to the higher-achieving West Covina High. Sure, we broke some zoning laws to attend, but if the Kennedys got ahead in part by dealing with the Mafia, and the Bushes got ahead in part by dealing with Nazis, then us dealing with fake home addresses to attend a better school did not seem so bad. This was the early nineties, the beginning of the fight for school vouchers and charter schools in California. Public money was rapidly being privatized and leaving our public schools. My parents learned about using a fake address so I could attend a better school through family friends who were willing to lend a helping hand. Without knowing it, my parents and I were playing the system in the same way the system always plays communities of color.

That freshman year of high school, I did something truly illegal. The year was 1994, and I had just turned fourteen. I remember it well because my parents and I used to rent movies at a local video store called Video 94. It was one of those small video stores that stayed in business mostly because of those mysterious, prohibited videos behind the curtain of an adults-only room. If you are too young to know what a video store is, just imagine a grocery store with aisles and aisles of cereal boxes with your favorite movies on the cover, but you not being able to watch any of them because the cereal box you wanted was always rented out. You don't know the pain of not having "suggested for you" on your home menu, or having to read each cereal box one by one to know what the hell you were even renting, or having to take ten minutes to rewind a movie before you could even start to watch it. If you only grew up with the Internet and streaming, then I have no place in my heart for you. You don't know the horror of having your hormones run amok and only having blurry porn on cable TV to keep you company. Pornography was not a real thing for me or any kid my age in 1994. No kid I had ever met knew what was behind those curtains at the video store, but we were all dying to find out. Up until that point I thought pornography was what I saw in James Cameron's *The Terminator* when Linda Hamilton and Michael Biehn made love before the big climax (no pun intended) of the movie. If you must know, Linda Hamilton and Michael Biehn inspired me to masturbate for the first time in my life. You did not need to know that, but I feel much better that you do. I am disgusted with us both.

My dad forced me to accompany him to the Plaza at West Covina one Saturday morning. We parted ways in the parking lot. He was going to look at new vacuum cleaners to torment me with and I asked if I could go to Tower Records, since record stores were how teenagers wasted their time before the advent of TikTok, Spotify, or ADHD.

I walked around Tower Records, excited to see the new CD releases. Tower Records also had a small section that was prohibited for children. In other words, they, too, had an adults-only room with a curtain protecting it from nosy kids going through puberty. For some ungodly reason on this particular morning the curtain was open. I stopped dead in my tracks. Holy crap! The secured-off area was not secured off. I looked around to see if there were any adults around. There were none. It was just me and an open curtain. I stuck my fourteen-year-old body to the wall and stealthily made my way into the prohibited area. For the first time in my life I saw X-rated magazines that, well, made what Linda Hamilton and Michael Biehn were doing in *The Terminator* seem like *Sesame Street*. This was a big deal. This was Skynet launching a nuclear holocaust. This was pornography.

I do not remember how long I was in the prohibited area. It felt like a lifetime to a boy coming of age. I definitely grew some chest hair while in that forbidden room. I also lost my innocence that morning. I now knew where babies came from. Although I must admit that some positions did not seem appropriate for impregnation. I had to leave the area, and that particular magazine in my hand had to come with me. I looked around one more time, and still saw no staff members anywhere in sight. I quickly lifted my shirt and tucked that cold magazine inside my pants. I was still a wannabe gangster at the time, so I had plenty of room in my baggy jeans. I casually walked out of Tower Records, and as the sun hit my face, I could not believe I had stolen something. I had never stolen anything—not even a kiss! What's more, I couldn't believe that I had gotten away with it. I took a deep breath. This was going to be the start of a new era of puberty for me. That was when I heard someone with a deep voice say, "You want to put that back?" I turned and saw the Tower Records head of security, a fit rocker who looked like he had just gotten out of a Metallica concert, staring at me. I did not know what to do. I panicked, so I ran. The security guard yelled, "Stop him! Thief!" I ran faster. I had a great head start on Master of Puppets so there was no way the security guard was going to catch me. Then, out of nowhere, a tank of a man tackled me shoulder-first to the ground. The linebacker was just some random buff white thirty-year-old shopper eager to defend the honor of American capitalism. I hit the ground incredibly hard. The guy was twice my age and three times my size. I wish I could say I was angry at this random white dude eager to punish minorities who didn't know their place. But truthfully, I was just angry with myself. How stupid could I be to live up to two stereotypes? I was now both a thief and oversexualized. Damn. Why did I have to be young, broke, and horny?

I was escorted to the Metallica dude's lair. It was like a cave out of a *Batman* movie, if Batman was a sloppy, lower-class slacker. There were walls and walls of monitors, and the security guard's only job was to study each of them and wait for a stupid kid like me to try something illegal. He had watched me the entire time inside the adults-only room. I sat there in shame while the security guard waited for my dad to walk into the store. Once he did, I pointed him out on the surveillance monitor.

"That's him. That's my dad."

Ride the Lightning went to grab my dad. He escorted my concerned father to his poor man's Batman lair and proceeded to tell him what I had done. My dad did not look at me. Not once. He simply told the guy, "You are wrong. My son would never do that."

"I'm more than happy to show you the footage, if you like."

"I don't need to see the footage," said my dad, now visibly upset. "My son would not do such a thing."

"Why don't you ask him yourself?"

My dad refused to look at me. At that point, I felt it was my duty to tell the truth. I sheepishly said, "I did it. I tried to steal the magazine." I could see my dad's blood starting to boil.

Metallica dude took a picture of me and said I was never allowed back inside Tower Records again. He then handed my dad a one-thousand-dollar fine that we had one month to pay before he reported us to the police. My dad and I drove home in silence. I had never seen him so furious in my life. When we got home, he walked up to my mom and explained that I was going to military school. It was one thing to look like a gangbanger, but now I was behaving like one. My mom, who always did everything my dad wanted, shocked him by saying: "Absolutely not." My dad was taken aback. My mom had never gone against any of his wishes. When he said let's move to the United States, she went. When he said let's change careers, she did. When he said let's move to another city, she moved. But there was something he had never expected: my dad never expected that I was off-limits.

My parents got in a big fight that evening, and they did so in front of me so that I understood what turmoil my actions had caused. My dad pointed out that I had put them at great risk—that they could not have Tower Records reaching out to the authorities. I did not understand the magnitude of the risk my dad was talking about, but I did not ask because he was incensed. When you're a white, documented citizen this is a harmless teenage adventure, the kind of thing your dad brings up in your wedding toast to embarrass you. But when you're undocumented, it could be catastrophic and upend your family's life. My parents were well aware. I was not. The Tower Records fine needed to be paid and my parents did not have any money to pay for it. My mom, in a firm tone of voice I had never heard before, said, "He is not going to military school and that is final." She then looked over at me. She was not upset; she was more disappointed. Believe it or not, that hurt even more.

"Fine," chided my dad. "He won't go to military school. But he will pay for that fine because I'm not going to."

"He will," my mom said defiantly.

I was fourteen. How was I going to raise a thousand dollars?

My dad stopped speaking to me for a time. This was his psychological warfare. If he was angry at you, my dad would not even acknowledge your existence. That to me was worse than any physical beating. After a month of being ignored every day, you wished for a beating just for the attention!

One day, I walked around Video 94 and noticed that the return movies were piling up and the lines of customers were getting longer and longer. The family-owned business needed help, but the video store owner was an Indian immigrant. He was never going to ask for help. It was an immigrant mentality I knew too well from my father. So I waited until the last customer had left and walked up to him. "Do you need help?" Sandip, the video store owner, looked at me incredulously and inquired, "Are you eighteen years of age?" I steeled myself and replied, "I am." I most definitely was not. Sandip looked me once over and then asked, "Can you work at night during the week?" I said, "Yes, I can." I was not sure if I could, but I needed to pay the fine before the police were alerted. Sandip then leaned in and said, "I can only pay you cash under the table. Is that okay?" I grinned from ear to ear. "Under the table would be perfect."

I started working at Video 94 immediately. Granted, I got paid only $2.25 an hour, which was much less than the California minimum wage at the time, but this job was my path to redemption. My uncontrollable hormones had caused me to steal a porno mag, I got caught, fined, and was then forced to find employment to pay for my mistake. And I did all this without documentation. Do you understand why I hate teenagers today who have the Internet while going through puberty?

I got acquainted with the Video 94 filing and computer system rather quickly and I was great with the predominantly minority customers. I went to school all day, did my homework as soon as I got home, and then I walked to the video store for my night shift Monday through Friday. I went in at 6 p.m. and would get out around midnight. I did this every school night. The reason the video store was open late was because we had a huge wave of single men who would come after hours to rent pornography so they would not be seen by regular customers during the normal store hours. It was a bunch of single men in desperate need of the Internet. The irony was not lost on me that the reason I was there was because I was eager to peek behind the curtain, and now I was in charge of restocking the entire adults-only area. I had access to all the porn I could ever want, but now I was too busy working to watch any of it. I would walk around high school exhausted with my eyes bloodshot red from the lack of sleep. So much so that the assistant principal pulled me aside one day and tried to convince me to stop doing drugs because, as he pleaded, "You're not a bad kid." I wish he would have told my dad that.

It was around this time that my cousin Joe came to live with us. Joe was eight years my senior but looked five years younger than me. He had been living in Utah for several years. He had even lived on a Native American reservation for a time. Joe had his heart set on being a professional snowboarder before an upside-down, helicopter-style snowboarding jump snapped his forearm in two, forcing doctors to insert a metal plate to keep his arm together. Joe came to live with us because he was in desperate need of medical supervision but had no health insurance. My parents, with their medical backgrounds, could provide him that with no HMO. Joe was not in good shape when he came to live with us, but little did we know he would end up healing us.

My dad did not want to take Joe in. Joe is my aunt Lupe's son and my aunt Lupe is my mom's older sister. Lupe was named after the Virgen de Guadalupe, but boy, was she far from it. My aunt Lupe, or Lupita mi Amor, as she would have me call her since I was a child, was the life of any party. Lupita mi Amor and my dad clashed a lot. She hated how my mom always did as he pleased. She felt that my dad did not deserve her younger sister. Lupita mi Amor is still the only person in history ever to throw an apple at my dad's face after an argument. Why would he ever want to take her son in?

When Joe moved in, I told him I liked his shorts. Without any hesitation, he gave them to me. I was happy wearing my new skater shorts. My mom, upset, pulled me aside and explained, "People who give you the shirt off their back always end up shirtless. Don't do that with Joe. He doesn't have much."

Joe took me on as his young Padawan. We shared an incessant love for the original *Star Wars* trilogy, but above all, I loved the music Joe listened to. My house was always filled with Spanish music or smooth jazz. Joe changed all that. One day, Joe was sitting next to the house stereo. "Come here," he said. "Check these guys out. They're called NOFX." The Cali punk sounds that blasted through our speakers engulfed me. NOFX, Pennywise, and Operation Ivy blasting through our living room speakers was exactly what I needed at fourteen years of age. My dad and I were still estranged. He and I did not speak much around this time, not after he tried to get rid of me via military school. The unity vibes and anti-authoritarian sentiments of Cali punk spoke to me. I started dressing more like Joe, a half American, half Ecuadorian who had spent his entire life bouncing from family member to family member's house. One night, as we were hanging out in the backyard drinking beers together, Joe pointed out, "We are the only two grandchildren that grew up with Grandpa." Before I was born, Joe had spent so much of his childhood with our grandparents, and he was my grandfather's favorite. "My German," my Tata would call Joe, due to his light skin and sparkling blue eyes. Joe and I had a bond that nobody could break. He was the only adult who truly understood me.

One night, when I came home late from Video 94, I found Joe and my dad in the backyard drinking beer, philosophizing on life the way Joe and I did. The sight was a little hard to comprehend and I was a little jealous. Only Joe and I drank beer and philosophized about life. I was fourteen, but as long as I had a full-time job, got good grades, and only did it at home, I was allowed to drink a beer with Joe. So what was my dad doing invading my space with my cousin? Technically, it was not my space. I did not pay rent, although I was working to pay off the fine. Then I heard my dad laughing and I was stunned. I realized in that moment that I rarely ever heard my dad laugh. Joe did something for me that I did not know I needed. He helped me see my dad as a person and not as the tyrant I had made him out to be in my head. Watching my dad hang out with Joe, enjoying himself the way I did, made me feel like maybe there did not have to be an ocean between us. That's when I told my dad, "I have all of it now. The fine can finally be paid off." My dad did not smile, but I could tell from his demeanor that he was pleased.

One particular Sunday at Video 94, a kind man from Indonesia sporting a gray beard, David, asked me why I did not have a car. David had seen me walk to the video store every evening on his way back home from his auto repair shop. He was an immigrant like I was, so he felt bad for me. "Haven't you heard the song 'Nobody Walks in LA'?" David was a mechanic, and he said he could get me a car to use. I told him I would think about it. It felt odd to be offered a car out of the blue, but the universe works in mysterious ways. Because a few days later, an unknown older white man in a blue sedan pulled up next to me as I walked to work.

"Do you want a ride?"

"No," I said as I kept walking. The man slowly kept driving next to me. Again, he asked, "Are you sure I can't just take you?"

"No," I now said forcefully. The man begrudgingly drove off. Not fifteen minutes had passed when the man pulled up next to me once again. "Come on. Get in. I'm heading that way anyway." Just then, a police car approached and the man drove off. I got to work and wondered if I was just making a big deal out of nothing, or if that man who I had never seen before truly just wanted to give a fourteen-year-old Latin boy a ride. That night when I saw David at the video store, I said, "Is that car offer still valid?"

I now had an old Nissan Maxima that I used to get to and from work. David trusted me to do the responsible thing with his car, so I did. My parents did not understand where the hell I got a car from. There was so much they did not understand about America. Did people just give cars away in this country? One night, while I was hanging out with my cousins Choli and Joe, I did the unthinkable. I took David's car out on a cruise. I had never gone out on a late-night joyride, and it felt exhilarating. To just pick up the keys and drive wherever you wanted at any time of day that you wanted. I had never felt that sense of freedom before. I parked at a gas station just as a police car pulled up right behind us. I quickly gave the keys to Joe and said he should drive since I did not have a license. That's when the cops started interrogating us.

"What are you guys up to? Where are you coming from?"

I was not nervous when they asked for the registration. The papers were all up-to-date. I only got worried when they asked for our license and discovered that Joe's was suspended. The police impounded the car right then and there. I felt horrible. David trusted me with his car and I stupidly had it taken away.

I had already paid off the thousand-dollar Tower Records

fine in full, two dollars and twenty-five cents an hour at a time. The manager must have been surprised that a fourteen-year-old kid could bring in a thousand dollars. I myself was surprised that I was able to do it! But now I had a new problem: David's car had been impounded. I went straight into saving the money to get the car out of the tow yard, which I did after a month and a half and a lot of overtime at the video store. But then the clerk at the impoundment lot informed me that I could not retrieve the car; the owner had to pick it up personally. I walked to David's house in shame and was forced to tell him the truth of what I had done. He listened compassionately and then thanked me for my honesty. Wow. I wished my dad had been more like him. David drove us both to the tow yard, where I paid to get his car out. When we got back to his house, he was kind enough to try to give me his car again. That's the type of person David was. But this time I told him, "No. I learned my lesson. I need to walk."

Becoming Zack Morris

Freshman year at West Covina High felt like a middle school holdover. All the troubled kids holding on to their gang-banging ways, who were simply in need of counseling, positive family reinforcement, and perhaps some behavioral therapy, were still around freshman year. As a natural introvert, I kept my head down and hung out only with my cousin Choli and my cousin Diane. Diane was Choli's older sister and was the smarter and more attractive version of Choli. As an upperclassman, Diane and her girlfriends had access to all the cool kid parties, as young attractive girls usually do. In fact, the first time I ever went to a twenty-one and older club as a minor was with Diane and her girls. I'm sure the bouncer knew we were all underage, but the ratio was worth the risk for him: four hot young girls and one dumb underage dweeb—*why not?*

Diane always looked out for me. She would sneak me snacks at recess, tell me who I should and shouldn't be talking to around school, and would vouch for me among her friends.

She was very sweet in that way. I would argue that Diane took better care of me than she did her own brother. Choli would agree, just not publicly.

By sophomore year, all the troubled freshmen had dropped out, been expelled, or sent to continuation school. In California, continuation school was an alternative high school diploma program predominantly filled with Black and brown kids. Continuation schools were essentially scholastic purgatory at local school districts. You never wanted to end up there. With all the gang-affiliated students gone, and when left to my own devices, I turned out to still be a big nerd at heart.

Choli fell in love early in our sophomore year. Overnight, I lost my partner in crime to Sandra, a charming half Mexican, half Thai, and full home wrecker. Without my cousin, I was all alone in this new teenage wasteland, and I didn't even know who I was. I was an immigrant, slightly bookish, ex–wannabe gangbanger who equally listened to the Beastie Boys and Carlos Vives. I didn't know what clique I belonged to at school. In San Gabriel Valley in the mid-nineties, the cliques available to me were the ravers, the taggers, the rebels, the jocks, the few remaining scholarly cholos, and the cool kids. I was none of these at the start of West Covina High School. Luckily, I found friends who felt the same exact way.

Sal, Napo, and Tommy were at the core of my school family. All the leading national research shows that students from marginalized communities cannot begin the learning process until they have created a family and a safe space in the classroom. That's what these three guys did for me without even knowing it. The four of us became like brothers, and as an only child who was always looking for siblings to bring into my life, these dudes were exactly what I needed.

Sal, surprisingly, was raised an only child just like I was. He grew up in an apartment most of his life like I did, and was a sweet dude that everybody wanted to make their friend. Sal's love of music was what united us. At the time, Cali punk was having a moment. You could always find Sal and me listening to Sublime, the Offspring, No Doubt, or Rancid. You could also find us outside of Tower Records on the weekends waiting in line for Ticketmaster to open so we could be the first to get Rage Against the Machine concert tickets. Rage Against the Machine was a perfect band for Sal and me: a Mexican American lead singer and a half Kikuyu Kenyan guitarist exposing us to social justice for the first time in our young lives. We didn't have the words for the cause of our teenage angst, but Rage Against the Machine definitely provided the lyrics. Our favorite pastime was to find rare VHS tapes of the band performing in backyard parties so that we could watch them over and over in a loop, always imagining being there, cheering them on.

My buddy Napo was half Mexican and half Guatemalan. If your prejudices made you believe he would be twice as short, you would be racist-ly mistaken. Napo was one of the bigger and more imposing dudes in our class. Napo's problem, however, was that he was all heart. I used to wonder, *Why be that big if you're just going to be kind to people?* It felt like it was a waste of a dominant body. In ancient times, Napo would have smashed his way to respect. Napo had immigrant parents who worked as much as mine did, which was how we connected initially. He and I were both different sides of the same "first-generation" coin: he as a child of immigrants, and I as the first foreign-born member in my family to be American. Or at least, so I thought.

Tommy, on the other hand, was a closed book. He was tall, very opinionated, an avid reader, and a huge lover of the Beatles. Or "los beet-less," as my mom would mispronounce. Tommy's dad listened to a lot of classic rock, so Tommy adopted the habit. His dad always worked on classic cars and lowriders, so Tommy drove a black '81 Monte Carlo. Tommy was also big into new wave and The Smiths. It would be like pulling teeth to get Tommy to open up about himself, but when he did, it was like a universe exploding into existence. But those deep conversations with Tommy—with any of my friends—happened only around alcohol.

Drinking at such a young age is perhaps the one factor that united us all, Choli included. We hung out with the cool kids early on simply because we could drink more than they could. Alcohol seemed like a rite of passage for American high school students. At least it was for us at West Covina High School.

One Saturday night our sophomore year, the guys and I decided to drive down to Balboa Beach, which was close to an hour away. The plan was to drink and listen to music next to a bonfire. There were a few other high school students there, but the trip was simply meant for the five of us to get drunk by the ocean. Up to that point, we were the beer kings. If it was good enough for the semi-nomadic Natufians thirteen thousand years ago, then it was good enough for us! We had never met a brand of beer that we did not like—Natural Light and Mickey's, included. But on this night, a rebel kid decided to bring a bottle of Jack Daniel's to the beach. Eager to play a cool guy, I challenged the rebel to see who could do more shots of JD. "It's on," he said, determined to expose me for the fraud I most certainly was. I had had tequila shots at a family party before. *How different could it be?* I wondered.

The first couple of shots weren't that bad. They only burned my throat a little. The next several shots were a little more difficult to swallow. My stomach was not happy. By the time we got to ten shots, I was feeling light-headed, but I didn't want the rebel to know that. We kept going. As hard as we tried, we didn't seem to make a dent in the Tennessee-labeled bottle. The rebel and I finally called it quits at sixteen shots each. We had clearly had enough. With me barely able to stand, the bonfire was now over. Choli helped me stumble back to Tommy's black Monte Carlo when the three of us were suddenly confronted by a police squad car. Visibly, I was the drunkest of us all. Choli and Tommy told me to play it cool as the two white officers instructed us to sit on the curb and proceeded to ask us a series of questions:

"What were you up to tonight?"

"Where are you guys from?"

"Have you had any alcohol this evening?"

Annoyed and completely inebriated, I slurred back, "I wss jest drankin' wit' my fronds, gawd!" Tommy quickly cut me off and apologized to the police officers. Luckily, he had barely been drinking and was simply eager to go home. I didn't blame him. It was 11:00 p.m. and Tommy still had a long drive ahead of him. Shockingly, the cops let us go. Maybe Tommy's Caucasian last name was a blessing for us all. The only thing the cops said to Tommy as we left was, "Please get him home immediately."

We didn't drive more than ten minutes before the back of Tommy's car started spinning. I was now feeling the full effect of the Jack Daniel's. We were on the freeway when I begged Tommy, "Please pull over!" The rest is a blur. I thought I made it out of the Monte Carlo in time to vomit. Apparently, I simply popped my head out of the window and let my stomach handle the rest. I came in and out of consciousness throughout the drive back to West Covina. I remember that one moment we were driving on the freeway, and the next we were at a gas station as Tommy used a squeegee to clean my puke off the side of his car. When I came to a third time, we were in front of my house, and Tommy and Choli were arguing about what they should do with me.

"I'm not going to take him home—my parents'll kill me," said Choli.

"Well, I can't take him to my house either," replied Tommy.

Out of fear of getting grounded, neither of them wanted to take me back home with them. Dropping me off and wishing for the best seemed like the only possible alternative to them. If one of us was going to be grounded, it definitely had to be me. Choli and Tommy both struggled to get me out of the car and to the front door, where they propped me up against it, rang the doorbell, and took off running. The last thing I remember hearing were the car tires screeching away.

My parents were hosting friends at the house that evening. When she heard the doorbell, my mom figured it was me. She happily opened it and I came crashing down on our tile floor. My mom gasped as I quickly got up, balanced myself the best I could, and politely waved at my parents' friends. I wobbled to my room and plopped down on my bed. Like the back of Tommy's car, my bedroom also started spinning. Always the medical doctors, my mom and dad rushed in and started checking my vital signs. They worried they would have to take me to the hospital to pump my stomach. My dad assessed the situation and came to the realization that I was going to be okay. They gave me water, helped me remove my vomit-covered clothes, and even made me eat some bread to help soak up the alcohol within my system. Even as intoxicated as I was, I was clever enough to defend myself before my parents: "You always taught me never to do drugs...but you never said anything about alcohol!" Now safe at home, I finally passed out.

The next morning, I was in huge trouble. I knew my dad would be upset, not just because I put myself in great danger by getting this drunk in the streets, but because I had made him look bad in front of his friends. He glared at me as I stumbled to the kitchen table and asked me what had happened. I confessed to having taken sixteen shots of Jack Daniel's. He couldn't believe how stupid I could be. He grounded me for four months. I guess it was one week for every shot. I was only allowed to leave the house to go to school and to go to work. The real punishment, however, should have been me being forced to smell Jack Daniel's every morning. Nobody can bring that brand of American whiskey within a five-mile radius of me to this day. I will throw up.

Outside of alcohol, the other thing that united Sal, Napo, Tommy, and me was the fact that we all had to start working at a young age. A lot of our friends didn't have to find employment during high school. Not even Choli. But Sal, Napo, Tommy, and I did. Sal worked part-time at a pizza shop. He worked under the table just like I did at the video store. Tommy had his worker's permit and had a part-time job at the mall after school, selling pretzels. Napo, on the other hand, was destined to learn the family business: landscaping.

A lot of kids at school liked to make fun of Napo because his dad was their gardener, completely unaware that Napo and his dad actually had more money than they did. The landscaping business in Southern California was always persistent. So much so that I asked Napo if maybe he and I should start working at landscaping together on the weekends. Napo thought it was a good idea, so he asked his dad, Ramon, an older but still very fit Mexican man from Zacatecas, if he would give the two of us a shot as workers. Ramon chuckled at us and in Spanish said, "Okay, let's see what you two got."

Napo and I showed up early to work together at the first site in South Pasadena. The house was big and there was a lot of landscaping work to do, but Napo and I didn't do any of it because we didn't know what to do. We helped with the trash and hauled some manure bags back and forth. But that was about it. We got in Napo's air-conditioned 4Runner and headed to the second house, which was smaller so we thought it would be more manageable. But the work turned out to be more complicated. The assignment was to put in some new plants along with a new sprinkler system. Napo and I dug where we were told, but we were both very confused. For all I knew, sprinkler systems were aboveground. By the third and fourth houses, it was evident that Napo and I were just getting in everyone's way. When we broke for lunch, Ramon bought us two delicious burritos, and suggested that we go home. Napo and I could not have been any happier. Outdoor labor was not for me. I was more suited for the video store.

I spent most of that high school year grounded. If my dad and I were home at the same time, I had to find busywork to do: wash the dog, vacuum the house, wash the dirty dishes. When he wasn't around, I basked in the glory of being a lazy American teenager. I snuck in TV whenever I could. It was on one of these days that I discovered reruns of the classic American sitcom *Saved by the Bell*. The series was about a charming white kid in high school who was always scheming with his group of friends. There was an ethnically ambiguous buff kid named A.C. Slater, played by Mario Lopez, who should have spoken to me. But instead, I was under the spell of Zack. That ease that heteronormative kids have, accompanied with that charm that white privilege gives you, topped off with that fake bleached-blond California hair...Zack Morris was everything I wanted to be.

Life was monotonous for me entering my junior year. I would go to school, get home, do my homework, go to work, and then be grounded most times in between. I wasn't happy. My life did not look like that of any of the American teenagers I saw on my TV. They seemed very happy. That's when I decided to take matters into my own hands. I didn't want to live in this broke Hispanic barrio story. I wanted to be Zack Morris, and I wanted West Covina High School to be just as fun as Bayside High. There was an episode where Zack joined the drama club, so I decided to audition for drama class. In another episode, Zack formed a band. (Who can ever forget the Zack Attack hit "Friends Forever"??) Well, Sal and I formed a band as well. We only played one song on repeat (Pennywise's "Bro Hymn"), but it was a band nevertheless. Zack played varsity sports, so I decided to play varsity sports. Granted it was soccer, but it was a high school sport nevertheless! If Zack Morris did it, then I tried it on for size. And it worked. High school was starting to be fun.

Believe it or not, I even dyed my hair blond. And for the first time in my life, I passed for white. It was strangely exhilarating. Girls started talking to me more. Teachers started helping me out in class. Law enforcement was even more courteous to me. It was bonkers. I was in an upside-down, bizarro world where I was no longer the edgy ethnic guy. Strangers treated me differently, so I started to behave differently. I became more wholesome and personable simply because people started interacting with me in that way.

At the video store one evening, an older customer I did not

get along with because he always spoke down to me with a condescending tone of voice approached me and said, "I really don't like that Latino kid who's here on the weekends. He's very rude. Can you please give that message to the owner?"

I was the Latino kid!!!

Holy hell.

This older customer did not recognize me whatsoever. "I will definitely inform the manager of your feedback," I responded with no intention of definitely informing the manager of his feedback.

Being Zack Morris made my life so much better. I had no road maps as a first-generation American student. I went through the public school system a little disheartened by the way it felt uninteresting and not the least bit engaging. At times it just felt like government-run day care. My teachers didn't expect much from me. Then again, I didn't expect much from myself. But everything turned around when I realized that nobody was going to create the reality I wanted, so I had to do it myself. I willed the high school experience I wanted into existence, and a cocky white kid on TV helped me do it.

The Big News

Since I lived far from the high school I attended, on the days that none of the guys could give me a ride home, I would have to wait for my dad to pick me up. He was down to one job (down from his regular two jobs), so he had the time to pick me up every other day. Did he want to? Absolutely not. And he would show his disdain by coming very late. I was upset to be the very last student at school on those days—even the janitorial staff who locked up felt bad for me. In my dad's defense, he always did pick me up. But he was like a cable service technician: the time window would be anywhere between one to four hours of the regularly scheduled time.

Entering my junior year of high school, I finally decided that I was going to get a driver's license. And that had to start with a driver's permit. Napo, Tommy, and Choli were all driving by then. Why couldn't I? I decided to sign up for the after-school driver's permit class, and I did so without telling my parents. I was afraid they might say I shouldn't.

The class was fun, but only because I took it with Sal. We goofed around a lot as we learned that the most important part about driving was to always be safe. When in doubt, just do the safest thing. Well, that felt simple enough. Automobile driving was one simple DMV test away.

Choli and his girlfriend, Yoko (I mean, Sandra), joined Sal, Napo, Tommy, and me. We became a tight crew inside and outside of school. Sandra eventually brought all her girls over to be part of our inner circle: Denise, Jessica, and Maria Jose. I developed a crush on Maria Jose (or "MJ" as I would call her) since the first day I saw her. A fair-skinned Mexican American with jet-black hair, MJ was a nineties girl who loved eighties music. She was like a sarcastic Snow White, if Snow White was really into Depeche Mode.

MJ and I became friends. I never told her I liked her. We would hang out and be emo before I knew there was even a word for it. We would drink, laugh, gossip, but always with one another. It was so obvious that we liked each other, but neither of us would make the first move. After school at a friend's house one day, I was teaching MJ how to play pool in the garage. When my friend's mom came out to check up on us, she even rolled her eyes at how obvious we were.

It took me forever to kiss MJ. We did so at a party. We were both highly inebriated. I can't remember who made the first move—it just happened. Alcohol had always done that to me. It made me more confident than I usually was. Alcohol gave me a weird sense of euphoria.

In driver's ed, Sal and I were shown a video of what

happened to a real-life victim of drunk driving. The video was gruesome and got its point across. I was saddened by the sudden realization that I may no longer be able to drink once I started to drive. But it felt like a fair trade to me. I couldn't wait to take MJ out on a date, just the two of us.

After our driver's ed course was over, we were all given papers for our parents or guardians to fill out. We were one step away from getting our driver's permits.

The evening of the big news, I walked into the house holding my driver's permit application. I was eager to take MJ out for a drive, preferably to the top of a hill with a beautiful view. I was always a romantic at heart. I handed my dad my driver's permit and asked, "Can you please sign this for me?"

My dad read the DMV paperwork and looked over at my mom, who stopped cooking her world-famous *seco de pollo* and took a seat next to my dad. Things started to feel off.

"We need to talk," my dad stated plainly.

Concerned, I took a seat. "Is something going on?" I said. "Is Grandma okay?"

"Rafa," my dad said, searching for the right words, "you don't have a social security number."

"Huh. Why?"

"Because. We told you. We're . . . illegal."

What! Illegal? I didn't know what he was getting at. So many things could be illegal. Driving over the speed limit is illegal. Insider trading is illegal. Singing "Happy Birthday" is illegal because it's trademarked. Drinking alcohol under the age of twenty-one is illegal. Shit, maybe I *was* illegal . . .

I looked over at my mom for clarification. She softly nodded her head. "We don't have papers."

"*Wait...we're illegal*," I exclaimed, now realizing what my parents were driving at.

Since no human being is illegal, I was clearly using the wrong terminology back then. But this was before the DREAMer movement. It was 1997 and all I ever heard on the news was how Get-Off-My-Front-Lawn Lou Dobbs would vilify undocumented workers. In Spanish, my parents never referred to themselves as "illegal," which is why I didn't understand the gravity of our situation until this very moment. Nobody I knew in small-town West Covina, home of Troy Aikman and Joan Jett, ever used that word. The most I ever heard my parents say was *"No tenemos papales,"* which translates to "We don't have papers." My young mind always assumed we would address whatever problem we had by simply...getting papers. But now my dad pointed out that we were "illegal." That was like an end-of-the-world-comet hitting my frosted-tipped head.

I struggled to make sense of everything. "We didn't cross a desert," I tried to rationalize. "We flew here—and it was economy plus, if I'm not mistaken!"

My mom calmly explained that we came on tourist visas but then overstayed. She said this while making me chamomile tea. She always knew how to relax me. My dad added that they had applied for our permanent residencies eleven years ago and had hoped we would have gotten them by now. I didn't know what a permanent residency meant, but it sounded pretty self-explanatory since I wanted to permanently be residing in the only place I'd ever known as home.

I started to get nervous. I was...*illegal*. What did that even mean? I didn't feel illegal. I felt pretty damn American. The chamomile tea was delicious, but not working. How would I ever join the Campus Republicans now? That's when it dawned on me. "Wait, how do you two work if we're illegal and we don't have social security numbers?"

My mom and dad looked at each other again. "Well," my mom lamented, "we don't have papers, but you're the only one with no social security number."

WHAT.

THE.

FUCK.

I was already freaked out that I didn't have a green card, but I didn't have a blue card either? I started to feel dizzy. My mom asked if I wanted more tea. She knew damn well I wanted more tea. But I was upset, so I said no. I got up and started to pace around the room. This made no damn sense. I knew that at sixteen and a half, I was barely legal, but this was preposterous.

"I can't be illegal," I demanded. "How am I going to apply for financial aid to go to college if I don't have a social security number? Oh my God—can I even go to college if I'm not legal? I need to become legal!"

"We're still waiting for our three green cards," my dad said with fake hopefulness. "Maybe they'll come in before you graduate." The tremor in his voice assured me that he didn't believe what he was saying. And for the first time in my life, my dad allowed me to talk back to him.

"You ruined everything!"

Moments later, I was sitting on my bed, wallowing in my own self-pity. I didn't know of any other illegals. How could I be one without ever knowing it? I felt betrayed by my parents. I was forced to leave Ecuador for their dream of becoming doctors in the States and now was paying the price for that dream. This was ridiculous. I looked up at my poster of Pamela Anderson and for the first time thought, *I'm even too depressed to masturbate.*

Rolling Papers

As much as I liked to imagine myself as punk rock and counterculture, I was always a pretty straight-edged kid. I had a few run-ins with the law, but it was mostly teenage stuff. I would get upset if my dad drove over the speed limit or if my mom took too many samples at Costco—and she *always* took too many samples at Costco. Sure, I drank while underage, but that just felt like a SoCal rite of passage. The early-onset alcoholism did not take away from the fact that I was an honor roll high school student who also held down a full-time job. The news of being "illegal" was too much for me to digest. In times like this, I usually turned to episodes of *Saved by the Bell* for guidance. But in this instance I didn't know what to do because there was no episode of *Saved by the Bell* where Zack gets deported!

My parents and I didn't broach the subject of our immigration problems again. My dad and I were always good about not talking about the things that really bothered us. My dad would walk around the house like a silent assassin. If something bothered him, or if he knew something bothered someone else, he would go quiet and vanish from any interaction. And so we began ignoring each other.

Outside of my dad, I also began alienating my friends. MJ and I drifted apart. Our relationship was a casualty of a lot of bitterness from the news I had just received and teenage hormones run amok while undocumented. I stopped hanging out with her or anyone not inside my direct inner circle. I, of course, spoke to Napo and Sal about my predicament right away. Or at least, they forced it out of me.

In the quad at school one morning, Napo and Sal noticed that I was uncharacteristically silent and asked me what was wrong. I didn't know what to say, or if I should say anything at all. Would Napo and Sal judge me or think any differently of me if I told them my secret? They were my brothers, but would I be putting them in danger if I told them the truth of my legal status? After a moment, I finally fessed up that I had something important to tell them.

"Is it about Ross and Rachel breaking up because I'm still in shock," said Napo.

I didn't know what they were talking about. That's how devastated I was by the news my parents had given me—I'd totally forgotten to tune in to the episode of *Friends* that began the "we are on a break" era. Next time give me a damn spoiler alert, Napo!

I somberly said that it wasn't about Ross and Rachel. I took a deep breath and finally let out: "I have no papers."

Sal looked around to make sure the coast was clear and then asked: "Like rolling papers? 'Cause I can get you some."

I laughed. Sal could always make me laugh no matter how much I wanted to wallow in my own self-pity. I told the guys what my parents had shared with me. I told them that I was not legal.

"My uncles don't have papers and they're doing fine," Napo said nonchalantly.

I had met some of Napo's uncles. They all had been in this country for over two decades. I didn't realize they didn't have papers. Somehow they managed to buy houses and drive nice cars and—more important—were able to provide for their families. Napo put his hand on my shoulder and made me feel like things were going to be okay. I looked up at Napo, who was much taller than me, and smiled. He made me feel normal again.

Napo began working with his dad more. Post our day-laborer-for-a-day debacle, he slowly started taking over the reins of the family business, and without telling his dad, he included our house in his route. In other words, Napo gave us free landscaping services. Ramon and his crew would come over once a week to tend to our modest grass. I wondered if these workers didn't have documentation. I asked Napo about it, and he said, "Nope—all of these guys are good. So is my dad." Wow. It turned out that our gardeners were more legal than us. Our gardeners, by the way, that we were not paying for.

My dad and I spoke less. We began to not understand each other at all. Unfortunately, we became a pale imitation of what we once were. Long gone were the elementary school days when we would try to play baseball together. I felt uncomfortable being home when he was around. I eventually asked Napo if I could move in with him. He loved the idea. He had older siblings he didn't really grow up with, and wanted nothing more than to have a brother his age at his house. But he knew we had to run it by his parents first. One evening, Napo and I went to speak to his mom and dad: Rosario and Ramon. Ramon and Rosario were a true immigrant success story. They loved each other dearly, built a large family together, created a small business from scratch, and happily grew old together. Like my parents, Ramon and Rosario always took in outsiders. Our homes were like revolving glass doors of aunts, uncles, cousins, friends, godparents, and perhaps a few coworkers. It was in their nature to say yes to my request. But Ramon surprised me when he said, "No." Ramon clarified that they liked me very much and that they would love to help me out. In fact, his and Rosario's house would always be open to me. But I had a mom and dad. Ramon clarified, "Any decision to move in would first have to be approved by your parents." Since I knew my dad wouldn't agree, Napo and I just left my request at that.

As junior year came to an end, I started drinking more. I couldn't get a driver's license. I couldn't get a work permit. But I could get someone older to buy me alcohol. I stayed out late longer. In my head, I thought I was sticking it to the man because what illegal immigrant wouldn't be out late drinking just to antagonize authorities?

Rolling Papers

I came home late one night drunk to find my dad on the couch watching an action movie, as usual. This was his nightly routine. He would watch movies until about 2:00 a.m., and would always be up when I got home. It was an awkward nightly interaction where we both avoided communication. This time when I walked in, my dad turned off the TV and got up from the couch. Without looking me in the eyes, he said: "At least now you know why I always wait up for you." He headed off to sleep, while I stood drunk and undocumented by our front door.

The American Revolution

My mom gently knocked on my bedroom door. She had just gotten home from work and wanted to talk to me. It was a few months after they told me the big news. Knowing her, she simply wanted to lift my spirits. But I was starting to like this new brooding version of myself. If you thought having no direction in life was hard, try having no direction while not being allowed to be in the country.

My mom walked in and sat on the edge of my bed. She looked at me and, with a twinkle in her eye, said, "I tried to tell you the truth about our status before, but then you wet the bed so I thought against it." I didn't think that was funny at the time, but I now appreciate a well-structured joke. My mom apologized and said she and my dad had had no choice. They thought it was best that I didn't know the truth. "Because," she said, "we didn't want you to grow up feeling different. Because dreams should not have borders."

Damn. That shit hit me hard.

"Please don't be so hard on your father. He's doing his best. He always wanted to make sure that you valued our sacrifices and hard work. But this one thing, we didn't think it was necessary for you to know so young."

My mom's pep talk worked. She and my dad had sacrificed so much to come to the United States and had been living with this distressing reality for so long. I had only been dealing with it for less than three months. I woke up the next day with a tiny spark under my ass. It didn't quite resemble fire— thank God because I would've had to get that checked!—but the spark was there. In 1997, nobody I knew referred to themselves as "illegal" or "undocumented." We simply said, "We don't have papers." That was me. I didn't have papers. But it didn't matter. I was still determined to be that all-American high school student I'd once aspired to be. My dad and I were still at odds, but that was okay. Whatever love I wasn't getting from him at home, I would just have to figure out a way to get from my fellow classmates at West Covina High.

My mom's pep talk forced me to put things into perspective. Anywhere else on the planet I might have been doing child labor in a sweatshop, or been a child soldier in some meaningless war, or worse—I could have been stuck all alone inside a cold, desolate cage separated from my parents. Again, it was 1997 and expressions such as "child migrant" or "DACA" or "don't @ me unless you're nasty" had yet to enter our lexicon. Beyoncé had not yet taken over the world, and having Bill Clinton in the White House was considered diversity in politics. I was a junior in high school, a promising sixteen-year-old student that looked like an aspiring MTV VJ, and the world could still be anything I made of it.

I was drinking with my cousins one weekend, thinking of the latest episode of *Saved by the Bell* I had seen in which Zack ran for class president.

"I'm gonna run for class president," I told Choli and Joe.

Having a spark of genius, Joe replied, "You should call your campaign Operation Rafa!" He, of course, was referencing one of our favorite punk bands of all time, Operation Ivy.

Soon after Joe's brilliant suggestion, Operation Rafa was in full effect. I gathered Choli, Sandra, Napo, and Joe, and we began making posters. Joe was a great artist and was therefore tasked with all campaign art design. Choli looked tough, so he was in charge of all campaign security. We had giant posters with a picture of a guy moshing next to the words "Operation Rafa." Nobody could possibly know what the sign meant, but it didn't matter. We knew.

Of course, we couldn't do the normal thing and hang up the posters during our free period—that would be so boring and un-Zack-like. No, we needed an explosive campaign announcement. Choli, Napo, and I snuck out of our houses late on a Sunday night and drove up to the school with our lights off. Joe didn't go because he was over twenty-one and we figured it would be best if he wasn't sneaking around a high school after hours. Choli, Napo, and I hopped the school fence and made our way inside the quad. For the record, this was the first time I had hopped any fence in my life.

The guys and I ran around the school, each holding our

own tape and posterboard. We plastered campaign posters all over the school. They were up on the gym entrance, right outside the school cafeteria, on the wall to the principal's office—they were everywhere. Students may not have known who I was, but as of Monday morning, they were going to know my presidential campaign.

Monday morning, I was in the shower singing Céline Dion's "All by Myself" when I spotted an open bottle of shampoo. You really couldn't blame me. It was the first official day of my campaign, and I had a lot of pent-up energy to release. But unbeknownst to me, the shower window was wide open. So as I put the shampoo to work on something other than my hair, I inadvertently locked eyes with Ramon mid-stroke. Ramon diverted his eyes and yelled some Spanish apology, I screamed for Ramon to trim the hedges—and slammed the shower window shut!

The guys and I arrived at school and I found myself at the center of attention. A student walked up to me and asked, "Are you throwing a party or something?" Damn. I guess being cheeky on the messaging was not a good idea. Another student asked if Operation Rafa was a concert we were putting together. I got a little deflated. All that work for nobody to know what the hell we were doing. I should have taken a damn marketing class! That's when Sally, an Asian American wiz kid and the envy of all advancement placement students, came up to me and said:

"Operation Rafa. I like it. I'll vote for you."

Yes! The smart kids got it. Praise the Lord for smart kids! A few even gave me their endorsements on the spot. In the end, nobody really knew what Operation Rafa was, but they all knew they wanted to be a part of it.

I was thinking about my candidacy in my American history class, when my slightly neurotic but very thoughtful fifty-year-old history teacher, Mr. Demke, said something that shook me to my core. He was in front of his chalkboard discussing the Boston Tea Party and the colonies' protest of the British Parliament's tax on tea, when he looked directly at me and said: "That's why we had the American Revolution...because there can be no taxation without representation."

HOLY SHIT!!!

There can't be taxation without representation in this country. Of course! I was blown away by what Mr. Demke had said. He finally connected the dots for me. How did nobody else see this? My parents were "illegal" but they always filed their taxes. I know this, because they were always happiest when they received their tax refund checks once a year. My parents paid payroll tax and property tax and filed their state and federal taxes, and we were all forced to pay sales tax when we went out. But they were "illegal" and could not vote or be part of our political process. That meant that my parents—like all hardworking employees without documentation in the United States—were being taxed without representation! It is what the American Revolution was founded on, and yet this country was doing it to us.

Now more than ever, I was determined to win. I ran a very tough campaign. I was up against two overly qualified girls who had been involved in the Associated Student Body since freshman year. I showed up out of nowhere with crazy-looking posters and a cool catchphrase. I had no platform, just an incessant need to be loved by everyone. I was tailor-made for politics! The girls I ran against lobbied hard to get us to debate, but the school didn't have the time nor the resources. Students would just have to make up their minds via our posters and our friendly dispositions. My motto was easy: "I'm just one of you." Also, the current senior class president, Vanessa, a brilliant young woman of color, was my cousin Diane's best friend. Her endorsement sealed the deal for my campaign.

I won the election by a landslide. No runoff needed. No stupid hanging chads. I felt bad for my two opponents. They were better students than me and had been far more involved in school up to that point. It was as if I was literally taking all their jobs! For clarification, I didn't *want* to be president. I *needed* to be president. I ran because I was undocumented and I desperately needed the love of my community. I was never going to lose that election. To this day I wonder if I would have ever run for class president if I'd had my papers.

The Illegal Presidency

Not all my friends were concerned about going to college. They were all mostly eager to start making money for themselves as soon as the public school system set them free. Tommy was different. He cared deeply about his higher education. That meant that at the end of our junior year, Tommy and I worked tirelessly to get our university applications finished in time for the admissions deadlines. It was great to have a friend to go over all the paperwork with. My parents didn't understand any of the American college application process, or—quite frankly—if I could even attend college. I applied anyway. I tried not to think of the consequences. Tommy and I dropped off our completed applications in the mailbox at the same exact time.

As I entered my senior year, I finally came into my own. I allowed my natural hair to grow back. I couldn't work legally, I couldn't drive legally, I couldn't leave the country for legal reasons, but I was popular at school and that's all that mattered to me. I was the senior class president and almost everyone at school knew my name.

At home, my dad and I were still at odds with each other. My mom tried to smooth things out between us, but it was no use. We were like two alpha dogs living under one roof—we should've been kept outside until we learned to coexist! Not to mention that my dad's mood worsened when my seventy-year-old maternal grandma came to live with us. Post Tata's death, my grandma started spending months at a time with each of her children in California. These particular months in the fall were our turn.

As I checked myself out in my bedroom mirror one morning, my grandma walked in holding an aloe vera plant. She tried to apply some on my hair, but I was able to dodge all her advances à la Oscar De La Hoya. I've always prided myself at having pretty good footwork. While known as "Mami Viola" to everyone in the family, my grandma allowed me to call her Abuelita, a privilege she did not grant most of her other grandchildren.

"Abuelita, how do I look?"

"You look good," she said, a little disturbed. "But why are you putting all that processed junk in your hair?"

She feared I was going to lose my gorgeous wavy black hair that way.

"Embrace the curls," she said. My grandma tried to apply aloe vera on my hair again, but she couldn't reach my head fast enough. I was much taller and a lot quicker. "Fine," she said, finally giving up, "at least put it under your eyes so your skin glows." The aloe vera plant was clearly a cure-all for my grandma.

As she applied the cool, natural ointment under my eyes, I wondered out loud, "Why is it so important that I have good skin?"

"So you can attract a good girl and get married this year," she clarified.

I laughed. I was two months shy of turning seventeen. I didn't need to get married. "I'm only married to the game," I pronounced, hoping my grandma would understand my hard-core street vernacular.

"What game! Marriage is a holy covenant. And you should not wait too long." She then took a bite of her aloe vera plant, which she claimed was also good for digestion.

At school later that day, seniors were asked to attend a seminar on how to fill out the FAFSA: Free Application for Federal Student Aid. As the senior class president, I had to attend. I smiled through the entire presentation, knowing too well that I would not be able to complete the FAFSA myself.

Post Operation Rafa, I became well known around school. I was starting to be popular, and I loved it because it made me feel less of a stain on our immigration system. When Winter Formal came around, I was voted onto the court. One of the perks of being on the Winter Formal court was that you didn't have to pay for your own tuxedo as long as you did a catwalk fashion show for all the students at lunch. Celebrities never have to pay for anything, and I first learned that during Winter Formal.

I was subsequently crowned Winter Formal king at our first official school dance. If that wasn't bad enough, when prom came around later that school year, I was also voted onto that court. The teacher assigned to validate the results of the students' votes pulled me aside and a tad bit miffed said, "You got on the prom court, too, but no student is allowed to be on two courts." I knew she was lying because there were never any bylaws written to regulate student dance court voting, but I let it slide. I was technically already the king.

A week later, I received two important pieces of mail at my home. The first was from Columbia House offering me twelve CDs for the price of a penny. That seemed remarkable to me! Only in America could you get a music deal this good. The second piece of mail was a letter from the University of California-Irvine. I held my breath before opening their official communication. Being accepted by a major California university was the final piece in my puzzle of becoming an all-American student, and I had secretly been holding out hope that the colleges I applied to would see past my immigration shortcomings. I was hoping universities would accept me for all of my high school achievements. Come on! I was the Winter Formal king, the class president, and an honor roll student. *What university would not want me?* I thought, as I opened my letter only to find a message that stated: "You are our perfect candidate, but can you please send us your real social security number." Despite all my hopes and wishes, I was the all-American high school student with one small exception: I wasn't American at all.

My dad came home from work that evening and found me sitting at the dinner table depressed. The UC Irvine letter was open and lying just an arm's reach away from me. We would normally just ignore each other, but for whatever reason, he cracked open a beer for himself and sat down next to me. He picked up the letter, glanced over it, and then put it back down.

"I went to the social security office last year," he said with a softer tone than usual. "I told them that we never got a social security number for you when we first came to this country and that they shouldn't punish you for my mistake. They said there was nothing they could do. But they did give us a Tax ID Number for you."

"What is that?"

"I don't really know. I guess for paying taxes."

I listened intently, knowing full well that going into a federal building was one of my dad's biggest fears. That and being vulnerable.

"I came here to be a doctor," my father explained. "I was put on this earth to save children's lives. But I can't do that here. The American Dream that everyone talks about, it's not for me. Maybe it'll be for you. If not, we might have to go back."

That night, I had the worst dream of my life. I was in math class, feeling despondent and detached, when MJ of all people leaned over from the desk behind me and asked if I was okay. I didn't respond. I was upset. Why would any girl want to be with me now that I wasn't USDA certified? But then she whispered, "My parents are out of town. You want to come over after school?"

I snapped out of my funk and said, "Yes, yes I would."

At that moment, the classroom door slammed open and seven immigration officers barged into the room in full military gear, guns drawn, yelling: "This is an immigration raid—"

I woke up in a pool of sweat. A little disoriented, I looked around my room, relieved to know that it was all just one big nightmare. I glanced out the window and saw Ramon cutting the hedges. He looked over at me and then joylessly—almost knowingly—tipped his hat.

Campus Ministry

West Covina High School had a vastly multicultural student body where the cool kids were Asian American, the advanced placement students were African American, and the stoner-surfers were Latin American. Our student body did not endorse any stereotype. It felt like a place where everyone intermingled. Well, mostly everyone.

There was a group of overachieving, predominately white students at our school that were fascinating to me. They were highly academic, very polite, but they seemed—by and large—to keep to themselves. Not all of them, of course. Just the crème de la crème. As the senior class president, I had to interact with everybody. But my god was the white junior class president and her all-American cohort, a force to be reckoned with. Her name was Susie, and she was a wholesome soon-to-be valedictorian. Her family had been in West Covina for many years. I'm sure they were there long before it became as diverse as it was at this point. If there was a junior versus senior activity, Susie and the juniors would always win. The homecoming float, the lunch tug-of-war, the assembly cheer competition. They took high achieving to another level.

One morning, after our all-grade Associated Student Body meeting, Susie invited me to attend the school's campus ministry with her. Like 85 percent of Latin America, I grew up a Roman Catholic. Jesus of Nazareth was not someone I had asked for in my life, but he was someone engraved in my psyche. I knew how to recite every major Catholic prayer in Spanish before I even knew how to speak Spanish! The Christian Campus Ministry sounded like the English version of things I had traditionally grown up with.

I showed up to my first campus ministry meeting during lunch. It was held in my old wood shop class. As I looked around the room, I quickly realized that this was where all the high-achieving white students—and a few of the white-passing Latino students—met. The star wrestler, the star theater student, the majority of the student government, and Susie were all there. They were all surprised—even a little elated—to see me there. The guys all shook my hand and a few of the girls gave me hugs. It was a lovely and welcoming environment. They opened with a prayer, and then went straight into having a discussion about how secularism was a huge threat to our nation. *Huh*, I thought. That's interesting. I was listening to a lot of Rage Against the Machine and Public Enemy at the time, so I thought the biggest threat to our nation was the financial oligarchy that controlled the United States government, which consequently meant that we should really take money out of politics. *Secularism?* I had never considered that could be a huge threat to the United States of America. How naive of me. To tell you the truth, I didn't even know what "secularism" meant. But I really liked the positive energy when everyone was welcoming me to the group, so I went with it. "Boo to secularism," I said as I made a mental note to look up the word in the dictionary (no smartphones yet, remember) when the meeting was over. They then announced that they would be going next month to Tijuana to work with an orphanage down there. It sounded like a lovely trip that I wished I could attend, but for obvious reasons could not. Before I left, Susie invited me to attend Tuesday night Christian church. I was shocked. Church for me was always early in the morning, on Sundays, and always in Spanish. Tuesday night? "Yeah, it's so much fun," said a jubilant Susie.

"Sure, I'll go."

I went to Christian church and Susie wasn't wrong. Tuesday night Jesus church was fun. It was very lively and featured an in-house rock band. It was almost like a mini concert. It turned out a sea of white teenagers rocking out in a safe space to Jesus Christ, their lord and savior, was a great time. They were no Zack de la Rocha or Tom Morello, but the Christian band definitely redefined what church could be for me. We hugged one another. High-fived. It was delightful.

When I got home, my mom asked me where I had been. Ironically enough, she was working at the Della Martin Center in the Huntington Memorial Hospital in Pasadena at the time. Della Martin was a young woman from a rich family who thought she was mentally ill as a child and committed her to a sanatorium for life. Della was released at the age of seventy-three and inherited her brother's ten-million-dollar estate. The official reason for her commitment was because she was considered a "religious fanatic."

I told my mom that I had just attended "Christian church."

"That sounds lovely," my mom said, with some reservation in her voice because, to her, Jesus should always be experienced in Spanish.

Curious, I asked my mom: "What is the difference between Catholics and Christians?"

My mom thought about it for a second but didn't seem to know. "As long as everybody is worshipping Jesus, that's all that really matters."

"But aren't Catholics Christian?"

"Of course," my mom said, leaving me more confused than when I'd started.

I showed up to school the next morning with a big smile on my face. I was still high on Tuesday night God. I noticed that all the kids I saw at church the night before didn't seem so happy. They weren't smiling or hugging anybody—not even me. No high fives. The weight of the new morning seemed to have gotten them down. But...not even one high five? I ran into Susie and thanked her for inviting me. She was truly happy that I had attended. Then I asked her: "By the way, what branch of Christianity is the campus ministry?"

"We're just Christian."

"I know," I replied, "but what denomination?"

"None. Just Christian."

"Yes," I continued. "I grew up Christian, too, but as a Catholic. What is the campus ministry?"

Susie blinked a few times, baffled by my question. She then smiled—first smile of the day—and went about her business. Now curious, I caught up with my old wood shop teacher, the one who hosted the campus ministry meetings in his class. He was a jolly older white man with thick glasses he would wear only when doing woodwork. I asked him the same question I'd asked Susie. He proudly explained that they were Evangelical Protestants.

"Awesome," I said. "I was just curious. Oh, one last thing, why is secularism so bad?"

"The separation of church and state is not right. It's the reason for all of the moral decay in the White House."

My wood shop teacher was referring to the Bill Clinton scandal, where the president had coerced a young woman into having sexual relations with him in the Oval Office.

"Yeah, I get it," I said. I actually didn't get it. I was too young and there wasn't enough high-speed Internet at the time for me to research further. I thanked my wood shop teacher and went on about my day. I was a little baffled by what I was learning in American history class versus what the campus ministry was preaching. The Founding Fathers of the United States demanded secularism (i.e., the separation between church and state) exactly because they felt that was the key to strong governance. Going against secularism seemed un-American to me. But then again, I wasn't American, so who was I to judge?

At the Della Martin Center, my mom took an elderly white lady who was suffering from dementia on a walk. My mom always enjoyed the soothing, outside live piano music that some of the patients recovering from drug addiction would play. In the middle of their walk, the elderly lady turned to my mom, frightened. She demanded to know what she was doing—"You're trying to kidnap me, aren't you!" My mom tried to calm her patient down, but it was no use. The lady fell into an anxiety attack, grabbed a nearby metal ashtray, and cracked my mom across the face with it. The ashtray hit my mom between the eyes, cutting a major artery. Blood started to gush out of her face upon impact. Unable to see through the pain, she instinctively focused her attention on helping the elderly lady, as opposed to helping herself. It was now nearly impossible to calm the patient down with all of my mom's blood squirting everywhere. My mom could have sued the hospital. At the very least, she could have received worker's compensation. But she wanted none of that. She was an undocumented worker and too scared to fight for any of her worker's rights. But more than that, she was just happy that her patient was now calm.

At home, I was shocked to see my mom in bandages. I was upset that she couldn't go to a hospital. Instead, my pediatric surgeon dad patched her up at home. She insisted that she was okay. "We have to thank God that nobody was seriously injured," said my mom, her eyes now nearly swollen shut. As you may have imagined, my mom returned to work the next day with stitches, her face covered in bandages, and looking

like a North American raccoon. This was her life in the Della
Martin Center.

At school the next morning, I sat by the tree in the quad
reserved for seniors, thinking about my mom's bruised-up face.
I watched as the students from the campus ministry walked
around, not talking to anybody but themselves. It was high
school. We all kept to our own groups. I did, too. But something clicked for me that morning. I decided that I wanted to
do a better job at welcoming others into my circle. I didn't
want to act one way with the people I loved outside of school
and then another way with people in class. I needed to be better about being compassionate with everyone around me. My
mom was. She was clobbered in the face with a metal ashtray,
and yet showed great compassion to the lady who had caused
her so much pain. I still had so much to learn about trying to
create my own heaven on earth. A heaven, by the way, that
hopefully didn't require proof of citizenship.

Free Rafa

On a very uneventful spring night, I was hanging out in my room with Choli and Tommy. We weren't doing much of anything, but the weight of not being able to do things that normal kids could was dragging me down. That's why when Tommy said he had to go home, I replied: "I'll take you!" Choli and Tommy looked at each other, wondering exactly how I was planning to do that.

Acting as casual as I could, I walked into the kitchen and asked my mom if I could borrow her car. She was rightfully scared because I had no license, but at the same time she felt bad because she knew I was old enough to get a driver's license. I begged her to let me drive Tommy home: "Please—it's just down the street."

She caved.

Tommy lived ten minutes from me, and for five brief minutes it was the most exhilarating time of my high school life. I felt free. I felt like anything was possible, even being a regular

American teenager just dropping off one of his best friends at home. Then, police lights lit up my rearview mirror. We heard the wailing of a police siren. The guys and I looked at each other in panic. I had been driving the speed limit. There was no reason at all to pull us over. With no choice in the matter, I pulled my mom's car to the side.

The muscular white police officer walked up to my car, leaned into my driver's-side window, and flashed his flashlight past me and directly onto Choli's face, who was in the passenger seat. Squinting his eyes, Choli was confused as to what was going on. The officer started inundating Choli with a bunch of questions:

"What are you smoking? Where are you going? What did you throw out the window back there?"

For clarification, Choli was not smoking and did not throw anything out of any window. Like me, Choli was simply enjoying the spring wind as we drove through West Covina without a care in the world. But unlike me, Choli had a shaved head and a mean mug. And in the late nineties in West Covina, that meant he was a gangbanger and that was enough reason for the cops to pull us over.

Choli respectfully answered every question, explaining that he wasn't up to anything. This was clearly a case of racial profiling and the officer was after Choli. For a split second, I thought I was going to get away with not having a license. I felt terrible for my cousin, but he didn't run the risk of being deported like I did. I was secretly happy that all the heat was on him. When the cop realized he wasn't going anywhere with Choli, he gave up and stood up straight. Then he asked me for "license and registration."

Shit. My mom never told me where the car registration was, but I had seen enough movies and TV shows to know it should be in the glove compartment. Thank God I was right. I handed the registration to the officer along with my school ID, which was the only form of ID I had at the time. Well, that and my public library card. The officer stared at my big cheesy smile on my West Covina High ID and then sternly asked me for my driver's license once again. I had no choice but to confess that I didn't have one.

"Please step out of the vehicle. All of you."

We sat on the cold sidewalk with our hands behind our backs like criminal delinquents. It's true that my presence in the United States was questionable, but Choli and Tommy had not done anything wrong. They were good kids. It also helped that the guys had their drivers' licenses. It was just me who didn't have anything, and the officer couldn't figure out why. He got upset—"Why don't you at least have a California ID?" I didn't know what to say, so I apologized. I said I hadn't had time to go get it with all my work and schooling, which was partly true. I added that he could call my school to confirm that I'm a student there. It was seven thirty at night. I knew he couldn't call the school. I explained that it was my mom's car and she let me borrow it for a quick emergency. That I was actually on my way home. The officer didn't believe me, so he asked for my home number so he could call my parents. Shit.

As the three of us sat on the curb unable to speak to

one another, we saw a few neighborhood cars pass by, slow-ing down to look and pass judgment. I didn't care about any onlookers. All I cared about was that my dad had not gotten home yet. The full wrath of the West Covina Police Depart-ment was nothing compared to what my dad would do to me if he learned that I took my mom's car out on a joyride.

After twenty excruciatingly long minutes, the officer returned from his squad car. He said he spoke to my mom and that my story checked out. God, I love Latina mothers! The officer was going to let us go, but on the condition that Choli or Tommy drive since they were the ones with the licenses. I was elated. It was as if the universe was conspiring. For what? I had no idea. To keep me out of jail, I guess. Then the officer added, "But I am giving you a ticket for driving without a license and for driving with no insurance."

"How much is that for?" I wondered naively.

"I don't know. You'll have to check." The officer knew. He just didn't want to tell me. It was for a total of one thousand dollars. That seemed to be the going rate for being a teenager while undocumented: one thousand dollars. It was expensive not to have papers.

The next day, the boys and I put our heads together and came up with the stupid idea of throwing a party to raise the money. We had never thrown a party that we charged for before, but this seemed to be a good enough reason to start. It was designed to be a backyard party with a ton of alcohol for underage kids called: "FREE RAFA." We secured a buddy's house for the venue, we got an aspiring DJ (really it was just the kid with a large CD collection), my cousin Joe brought us the alcohol, and Sandra and the girls were kind enough to run the door, which was really just a fence to the backyard of a house.

The guys and I spent a week promoting the party at school. The promotion consisted of a hand-drawn flyer of me in jail with a large scary inmate hugging me from behind. The inmate, by the way, was modeled after the police officer who gave me the ticket. The smart kids at school wondered if these flyers meant that I was running for midterm elections or something. Smart kids can be so dumb sometimes. I clarified that, no, this time it was for an actual party.

As I sat with the guys in the large empty backyard, I was nervous that the party would not work. I was popular because I loved hanging out with all the different groups at school, but not all of them were alcoholics like us. I hid in the back of the house for most of the night. I heard some people arrive, but I couldn't tell how many. Again, it was a large backyard to fill. When my friends finally found me in the corner, they asked me what the hell I was doing.

"Everyone is looking for you," said Sandra.

Everyone? I stepped outside and discovered a large group of underage teens partying their asses off. They more than filled up the backyard. Everyone was there—even the smart kids. I was astonished. The boys and I had never thrown a party before, yet we packed that house. I knew right then and there that we'd missed our true calling of becoming club promoters.

We raised over a thousand dollars that night. We were able to pay for my driving ticket, the kid with the large CD collection, our buddy who let us use his house, and we still had enough money to take the crew to Boca del Rio (the most important taco stand in the West Covina area—period!). I couldn't believe how the entire school came to my rescue that night. To this day, they have no idea they were helping out an undocumented student in desperate need. I guess the hand-drawn flyers of me in prison with a large menacing white guy ready to take advantage of me touched everyone's hearts.

My school had my back. That true feeling of acceptance was exactly what I had been searching for since the day I discovered I wasn't "legal." It was at this time that ballots for the yearbook superlatives were released. It was time for us to vote on who was the "Best" at everything.

Some things fell into place naturally. Choli got Toughest Looking, Tommy got Most Opinionated, and Sal got Best Personality. I, on the other hand, demanded a lot of recognition. I knew I wasn't the smartest, the most athletic, or the handsomest guy at school. I didn't stand a chance for any of those categories. But there was one category that sounded vague enough for me to win: Best All-Around. What did Best All-Around even mean? No one knew, so I figured I had as much chance as anyone else.

I went into campaign mode one last time. I shook hands with the jocks, I waved at the color guard team, and I even kissed some babies (who belonged to the academically inclined cholas). But I was up against one of the coolest kids at school,

Daniel. Daniel was a light-skinned Hispanic kid, who was literally better than me at everything. He was a star basketball
player, on the principal's honor roll, which was a bigger flex
than the regular honor roll, and a classically handsome young
man. Daniel was also a kind soul. That was exactly how I
knew I could beat him. In the immortal words of George R. R.
Martin: "When you play the game of thrones, you win or you
die." Daniel had to die, metaphorically speaking, of course.

The War for Best All-Around was close. If Daniel had cam-
paigned at all, which he didn't, he would have definitely won.
Hell, if Daniel had had half the chip on his shoulder that I did
for being undocumented, he would have crushed me. But he
didn't. He was confident with who he was. I wasn't. Not at
that age. I had a secret that nobody outside of my family or
my boys knew, and the more accolades I won, the farther away
I felt that people would get from discovering the truth. I was
the Winter Formal king, an honor roll student, the senior class
president, and now Best All-Around. Sorry, Daniel—you'll
always be Best All-Around in my heart, just not anybody else's.

My high school counselor called me in for one last meeting. She was a kind and mature woman who cared deeply
about her students. Unfortunately for me, my assigned counselor was white, so I did not feel comfortable speaking to her
about my immigration problems. She informed me that two
universities reached out asking about my social security number. I fidgeted in my chair as I told her not to worry—that I
was on the case already. Comfortable with my answer, my
counselor then reiterated that I should definitely go to college:

"The time is perfect for students like you because of affirmative action." I didn't know what affirmative action was.

College acceptance letters started coming in. Around student government, the seniors were getting into Stanford, UC Berkeley, and UC Irvine. Tommy was accepted to his number one choice, Cal State San Diego, since he was determined to get out of the SGV. Choli would be a little closer, as he got into Cal State Fullerton. Running out of options, I began searching for alternatives to higher education and found a pamphlet about the California community college system. It was so cheap that I wouldn't need FAFSA, Cal Grants, or any type of government assistance that I wasn't eligible for.

The West Covina High administration asked me to give a speech at our graduation. I wasn't asked because I was the valedictorian. I was asked because it was customary for the class president to speak at the ceremony. I was ambitious, just not valedictorian levels of ambitious! I dreamed of standing at the podium and declaring that I was "illegal," explaining that those people you fear are only making our economy stronger, our workforce younger, and that their children are going to pay for your damn social security checks when you retire. But I didn't say any of that. I was too scared. Since I didn't know any others, I was convinced that I was the only undocumented student in the nation. I don't remember what I said at the podium. I'm sure it was similar to what Zack Morris said at his graduation from Bayside High. But as I looked out at all those shiny maroon caps and gowns, I remember being jealous. Sure they were listening to me, but I wanted to be like

174

them: to be able to graduate from high school with a green card and a social security number; to be able to finish my high school career and have the promise of a new American future before me. I had no idea what would happen to me after high school. Perhaps my dad was right and we would have to go back to Ecuador. I received a round of applause and then sat back down as a high school student one last time.

The day after graduation, I walked around the house in a daze. I felt lost. I didn't know who I was if I wasn't the class president. I walked into the kitchen as my dad read the newspaper that had a picture of Monica Lewinsky staring back at him. He read about the sexual scandal in the White House involving this very young woman (barely an adult) and he said, "American presidents are just as bad as the South American puppets they install." My future was uncertain, but one thing was clear: several presidencies had come to an end.

Machismo Facade

The summer I graduated from high school was the last time the boys and I spent together as a group. We kept in touch, but we weren't the tight family unit we once were. It was sad to say good-bye to all my friends who were heading off to college, a luxury I couldn't afford. It was difficult to watch everyone take their next steps in life while I was stuck at home. But I kept my game face on and wished all my friends the best.

Then 1999 hit, and my world was changed forever.

It all began the evening of February 24 as I sat down in my living room to watch the Grammys. The telecast had great performances by the likes of Madonna and the Dixie Chicks, but musical historians remember it most for Lauryn Hill's groundbreaking win for Album of the Year, the first time a hip-hop artist had won that coveted prize. However, the only thing the average American who watched it live—Latinos in particular—will ever remember of the 41st Annual Grammy

Awards was the man who would forever be known as Ricky Martin.

Ricky was performing "The Cup of Life" live in front of an English-speaking American audience for the first time. I was glued to the TV the second it started. My mom, who knew the song from Spanish language radio, rushed in as soon as she heard it begin. It was also the official song of the FIFA World Cup, which was why my dad joined us as well. If you were Latin American, you knew that song before the Grammys even aired. But like the rest of the United States, I was about to wake up to its performer.

The trumpets introduced him, but he wasn't revealed until one of his giant, shiny Pablo Picasso cubist set pieces dramatically flipped around. When Ricky started singing, it was evident that we were all witnessing a supernova in the flesh. He was a handsome young Puerto Rican who had a captivating voice, undeniable good looks, and an uncanny command of his lower body. My mom's jaw dropped. My dad shifted uncomfortably on the couch. I, however, could not be bothered. The way Ricky Martin danced salsa onstage, the way he sang with such glee, the way he had the entire audience in the palm of his hand . . . it was as if Ricky was redefining masculinity in front of our very eyes. He was shaking his hips in ways that Elvis Presley was banned from doing on TV just decades before. The audience at the event could not stop cheering for this multitalented Latino. I knew America was losing its damn mind because I was, too. I didn't look like Ricky, but I knew those moves were deep inside me. It's the music and the passion I grew up with my whole life. In 1999, Ricky Martin was the type of man I wanted to be: confident, talented, and unapologetically Latin. Every young woman I knew who watched the Grammys that night went crazy over him. Ricky Martin finally made me feel sexy without having to pretend that I was Zack Morris.

Ricky Martin kicked off what the media went on to dub "The Latin Explosion." Record companies couldn't find Latin American performers fast enough to exploit the Ricky Martin phenomenon. The Colombian Shakira, the Nuryorican Marc Anthony, everyone had crossover records in the works. Rising movie star Jennifer Lopez redefined herself as the singer J-Lo. Even Europeans, like the Spanish Enrique Iglesias, got in the game. The Latins in the music industry were exploding and I was going to do my damndest to take advantage of this newfound fascination with us. I wore tighter shirts. I bought an Enrique Iglesias beanie. I took salsa classes that I never intended on finishing. But it was no use. I would attend backyard parties with very little fanfare. I couldn't "She Bangs" my way into any girl's number. Nobody cared that I was Latin. Ricky Martin's sex appeal was not trickling down to me.

With the sad realization that I wouldn't explode like the Latinos on MTV, I finally forced myself to enroll at my local community college, Mt. San Antonio College. It turns out all my hard work in high school didn't mean much of anything once I graduated. Out of desperation, I applied for financial aid and was denied just as quickly for being undocumented. I was forced to pay for college out of pocket, which meant that community college was the only thing I could afford. My dad warned me that as long as I lived in his house, I had to go to college and pay for it myself. It turns out, community college was how you made cheap immigrant fathers happy. I was still working under the table at the local video store, so I could afford the community college tuition myself. It's terrible that higher education is so expensive in this country, and—worse—that it's predominantly minorities that end up in bankruptcy because of it. Nevertheless, there I went.

The majority of my West Covina High School crew went to Cal State Universities. Cal State Universities were cheaper than the University of California system: same academic rigor minus all the extra fees. Napo, Sal, and I, however, stayed put. The three of us trekked our way to Walnut, California, to attend the University of Walnut. There is no such thing as the University of Walnut! It was just how we referred to Mt. San Antonio College—or Mt. SAC for short. By the way, I don't advise anyone to text "Mt. SAC" to your college professor because your phone will always autocorrect it to "my sack." It is quite embarrassing.

My sack—I mean, Mt. SAC—was a bus ride away from my house. I spent most of my teenage years looking down at public transportation and at all the maids, nannies, older immigrants, and low-paid workers who had no choice but to take the bus. I was now one of them. It was difficult maneuvering my way through Mt. SAC with no social security number. When I first went to take my English proficiency test, they asked for it so out of desperation I made one up. Then when I went to take my math proficiency test, I forgot the number I used, and angry with myself, I made another one up. The result was that I had inadvertently made a bigger mess for myself. I had created two Rafaels at Mt. SAC: one who was good at English but bad at math, and the other who was good at math but bad at English. I remember sheepishly walking up to my remedial math college professor and saying I didn't belong in this class, to which he replied: "I know, son, nobody does." It was like elementary school all over again, which made sense since it was a remedial class!

It took me an entire semester to figure out the mistake I'd made. I knew there was a reason I was being blocked from taking higher-level courses. I was worried about talking to any college official for fear they might turn me into the authorities, but I had no choice. It was either overcome my crippling fear of sharing the truth about my immigration status or stay in community college until both Rafaels finished their AA's. I had to fix this two Rafaels problem. I took a deep breath and signed up to speak to a college counselor. I was assigned an incredibly caring Japanese American counselor named Audrey Yamagata-Nogi. Ms. Yamagata-Nogi had dedicated her entire life to helping the young aspiring minds that walked through the halls of Mt. SAC. Undocumented students were not common at this time. According to the future state bills that went on to support undocumented students like AB 540, there must have been others, but none of us were out. Therefore, I was paralyzed by the fear that I would be deported if I admitted to being one. I played dumb with Ms. Yamagata-Nogi, saying that I didn't know why I had no social security number. It was news to me. *Cough, cough.* But I was honest about having an Individual Taxpayer Identification Number. If you're keeping track at home: I was not allowed to be in this country, but as long as I was here, I needed to pay taxes. Again, the American Revolution was founded on the idea that there should be no taxation without representation. But I digress.

Ms. Yamagata-Nogi considered the situation. Clearly the federal government knew I was here if they had issued me a Taxpayer ID Number. But then again, what student does not have a social security number? I started to breathe heavily. I was now eighteen, and as an adult, I feared I ran a greater risk than when I was underage and in high school. But with a wave of her pen, Ms. Yamagata-Nogi fixed all my legal problems at community college with one simple solution: "I will give you a Mt. SAC ID number. Use this for everything while you're here." Ms. Yamagata-Nogi was taken aback by my reaction. In all the history of Mt. San Antonio College counseling appointments, I am certain no student ever did a victory dance upon receiving a Mt. SAC ID number. If she knew about my legal problems, she never once let on. Everything seemed to be back on track, for now.

Once I was able to unite both Rafaels, I had access to college courses that were transferable to the UC system. Because I was behind in my schooling by a semester, I started community-college-hopping. My cousin Diane was getting ahead in her classes at Cal State Fullerton by also going to Citrus College, a community college where her old high school counselor, Mr.

Burmingham, was the Citrus College English professor. Can you imagine needing to be a community college professor as a side hustle because being a full-time high school counselor did not pay enough? Like the old saying goes: those who can, do; those who can't, need at least three jobs to stay afloat while your *doing* robs the working class blind. I'm paraphrasing.

Using my Mt. SAC ID number as my social security number, I enrolled at Citrus Community College as well. The maximum college credits any student could take at one community college in a given semester in the state of California at that time was eighteen. By going to two community colleges, I was able to take twenty-four credits a semester. In other words, I had no life. Between college and the video store, my friends never saw me. Community college was burning me out fast. It was at this exact time that I enrolled in a third community college.

While all this was going on, my American life was in total limbo, even more so than before. My parents had hoped our permanent residencies would arrive before I finished high school, but they didn't. I was in community college buying time while the United States' family reunification program (or as the forty-fifth president called it, "my third set of in-laws") worked itself out. We were thirteen years into the process and still waiting. This immigration purgatory, the idea that I might spend another five years or fifteen years waiting for our petition to be approved, caused me to take every class in the course catalog, simply to take advantage of it in case I got deported. I simply went in alphabetical order. I took:

anthropology, biology, chemistry (I should have picked a different "c"), economics, geology, humanities, political science, philosophy, and theater. I didn't want to take the theater class. I feared that my neighborhood cholo friends would beat me up.

I walked into my first acting class with trepidation. My theater professor, an awesomely judgmental gay man who used to teach theater at Michigan University but who was happy to work in the California community college system because of the better pay and even better weather, assigned me a monologue from *A Streetcar Named Desire*. Luckily, I worked at a video store and found a copy of the old black-and-white movie starring Marlon Brando. I saw what he did with the words and then tried them on for size. I got in front of the class, and did what I had been practicing in the mirror for a few days. It was a thrill to perform in front of people. When I'd finished, my theater professor said that I definitely needed to audition for the school play. He said I was a natural. *A natural what?* I wondered.

I auditioned and got the lead role of our college's production of a Chicano play by Milcha Sanchez-Scott called *Roosters*, which was in part about a father returning home from prison and his young campesino son having a hard time accepting him back into the family. I played the son, but I was a complete novice to acting. It was one thing to follow an established blueprint created by Marlon Brando to get an A in class, but it was a whole other thing to do the handiwork of creating a character yourself. I didn't know what I was doing, so I took direction very well—eager not to look like an idiot onstage.

I would rehearse with my new homeboy Eddie, who despite looking like a local gangbanger, had studied theater all four years of high school. Eddie helped me with my memorization, with my blocking, and with intent. I was surprised to discover that acting wasn't so difficult for me, especially after having acted like an American for most of my life.

As opening night approached, I found it harder and harder to tell my parents about the play out of fear that my dad would get upset. Our relationship was just as bad as ever, and I didn't want to make it worse. He'd sacrificed so much to come to this country, and in return I wanted to be an actor? Give me a break. I'm upset at myself just writing about it.

Opening weekend was Mt. SAC theater program's greatest lesson in live events: always cast Latinos! Boy, did my family come out in droves. My family helped sustain that opening weekend on their own. My aunt Teresa, my uncle Ivan, my uncle Sergio, my aunt Lucha, my uncle Pete, my aunt Betty, my great-aunt Emma—everybody showed up! At the time, I was incredibly embarrassed that they were there. Now I realize how lucky I was to have such a large and loving family eager to support my stupid pipe dream. My mom and dad were present as well, of course, but I had only informed them that week that I was in a play so to them it was a one-off. Their response to my new interest in theater was not anything we had discussed up to that point.

The impromptu opening-night party for my family at my house was as last minute as some of my acting choices during the play. My aunts, uncles, and homies piled into our West

Covina condo. As always, the beer was flowing. We were still fighting for upward mobility, so hard alcohol was not a common practice for us then—it was too expensive. I was drinking with Choli and Napo when my dad pulled me aside. He was several beers in when he said he wanted to talk. My dad was not known as a man of the arts. As a pediatric surgeon, he was clearly a man of science. He would get drunk once in a while at family gatherings and bring out his old guitar, giving us all a glimpse of that South American high school student who could have had a musical career but whose father forced him into a career that was less *"estupido."* I thought perhaps this would be our conversation on this night: finding a career less stupid. I had been waiting for him to ask me why the hell I was pursuing theater. What he said next left me speechless...

"You were...good. Very good. And I know it must have come from all of our problems."

Wow. My dad thought my portrayal of a young man fighting with his estranged father was so believable that I must have been tapping into our real-life friction. Astonished, I then watched my dad do something he had never done in my presence before. He cried. My dad would cry many times in front of me after that, but this night was the first time he had ever done so in my presence. The machismo facade was slowly peeling off in front of my very eyes. I had never seen them before, as a child or as a young man: my father's tears.

I never once thought of my dad. I was too concentrated on hitting my blocking and finding my light to care about anything else, even the acting part. When my dad told me my performance was good and that it must have come from all the problems we had with each other, I remember thinking: *I was just trying not to forget my lines—ain't nobody thinking about you!* But I didn't say that. I thought it was important that my dad cry. I thought it was important that I cry with him as well.

I believe that blood is thicker than water, but that love is thicker than blood. Enrique was not my biological father, but he was always my dad. Like he said to me once during a fight when I was fourteen: "You don't have to love me, but while you live under this roof, you do have to respect me." That was our deal. All I had to do was respect him. I was an ungrateful teenager living for free, and all I had to do for rent was not be disrespectful. I can't imagine what he went through all those years. I'm sure that not being his blood made raising me and loving me that much harder. How difficult it must be to love a child who is not your own, and how complicated it must be to discipline said child. Luckily, we both had my mom's love to bind us together. It is not a hyperbole when I say that my mom was the glue that kept our family whole, just like my *abuelita* did for her immediate family before her. Nothing could have made this vulnerable moment with my dad more perfect. Two men brought together not by blood, but by love. Crying.

Many years later, Ricky Martin redefined what it meant to be a Latin man for me once again by coming out of the closet. It was a devastating shock to admiring Latinas all around the world, my mom most of all. But to tell you the truth, with an extraordinary global music career, engaged political activism, and a foundation that fights to end human trafficking, Ricky

Martin continues to inspire me to this day—sexy gyrating hips and all. Ricky spent most of his life building up the courage to publicly come out of the closet. I related to that struggle insofar that I was still trying to find the courage to finally come out of the shadows.

Stuck in Tijuana

After the closing night, my castmates in *Roosters* decided to take a trip together. They were going to Tijuana, Mexico, to let loose. They invited me to go, and I said yes. Stupid? Incredibly. But I couldn't say no to Maddie. She was one of my many costars and, up to that point, the most progressive person I had ever met. Not just in politics, but in her philosophy of life. My repressive Catholic upbringing didn't know how to handle someone who actually said what they were feeling.

Maddie was our de facto leader. The cast was already an eclectic group of people. There was Eddie, my cholo homeboy who was a secret theater nerd. There was Juan, the much, much older Mexican man who was a bit of a megalomaniac. There was Angie, the talented chola with a heart of gold. And then there was Maddie. Maddie was a phenomenal actress. Unlike the rest of us, Maddie wasn't Latina—she just played a different ethnicity. She was Scarlett Johansson before Scarlett Johansson (re: *Ghost in the Shell*). I loved hanging out with

Maddie before rehearsal and running lines with her. She was artsy and assured of herself. Nothing ever bothered Maddie because she was an incredible communicator. It wasn't just that she said what was on her mind, but that she said it in such a way that it never hurt anyone's feelings. When Maddie spoke to you, you knew she was going to be thoughtful, even as she was telling you off.

We were running lines together one evening when she caught me looking at her a tad bit longingly. I was developing a crush on her, but I never had much game, so I just kept my feelings to myself.

"You like me, don't you?"

"Umm...ah...I," I stumbled.

"It's okay," Maddie replied. "I like you, too. But we obviously shouldn't do anything until the run of the show is over."

Who says stuff like that! Maddie is who.

It turned out, Maddie was also sex positive. She had no problem talking about her needs and desires. It wasn't a taboo for her and her parents to talk about sex. In fact, she was much more responsible with sex exactly because of all her early sex talks with her mom and dad. Maddie could differentiate between love and sex, and could speak openly about both.

Maddie and I were intimate together shortly thereafter. But unfortunately for me, it was just a onetime thing. Maddie clarified that she only wanted to experiment sexually with me and nothing else. I didn't know how to take that. She was treating me the way guys would treat girls. I felt a little used. My eyes are up here!

By this point, I was exhausted from being afraid of my immigration status. Accepting the invitation to Tijuana was my way of saying, *I've had enough.* Also, I wanted to see if there was anything between Maddie and me. We had been intimate together but had never kissed. Her rules, not mine.

I was frightened about crossing the border, but I tried not to show it. I found comfort in how everyone in the group had gone before, and how they said Border Patrol didn't even check their passports. I was told that there were so many San Diego college kids crossing that everyone got waved through quickly. My goal was clear: to be mistaken for a San Diego college kid. We drove the three hours to Tijuana from Walnut, and nobody could figure out why I was so quiet. I was always the boisterous one of the group, so it was definitely out of character.

We arrived at the border, parked, and then walked over a pedestrian bridge. I saw a sign that read, "You are now leaving the United States." My heart sank. This was one of the stupidest things I had ever done. In fact, this was the very thing I had feared my entire life, and here I was doing it voluntarily. I was self-deporting. I closed my eyes and took some deep breaths. Worse than Border Patrol, I kept hoping that my parents would not find out about this.

Tijuana smelled different. It smelled more like car exhaust. There were a lot of taxis gathered at the border, eager for our business. We hopped in the safest-looking one and asked to be taken to Revolution Avenue, where a line of nightclubs resided. At this point in the night, the older Juan took over.

It was as if he was a regular down here. I badly needed a drink. Thankfully, the drinking age is eighteen in Mexico, so I was able to drink freely and openly. The funny thing about Tijuana was that, as I was promised, it was mostly populated by underage white kids from San Diego. There were hardly any Mexicans partying at the clubs we stopped at. I felt more out of place in TJ than I did at a house party in West Covina. After my first shot of tequila, I loosened up a bit. The worry of how I was going to get back into the country slowly faded away. And then I started to dance with Maddie and nothing else mattered. All I wanted was a kiss from her. No parents, no green card, no problem. I had the cast of my show, the tireless Tijuana nightlife, and an awful lot of legal alcohol at my disposal.

We hopped around from club to club. I felt like a big man because I wasn't worried about being carded for the first time in my life, plus I had some cash from my video store job that I was carelessly throwing around. Tijuana was truly as fun as everybody said it would be. Maddie was a little distant and flirting with some random military guys. She eventually came back to dance with us—and started paying attention to me once more. Maddie was hot and cold with me most of the night, but I couldn't be upset. She'd warned me ahead of time that she wasn't looking for anything serious. But now as she danced with me again, things were looking pretty promising on the romantic end. Then we had to head back.

Standing in line at the border to come back into the United

States, my heart started pounding. I sobered up rather quickly. The reality of my situation was hitting me like a baseball bat to the gut. I was distressed standing at the San Ysidro checkpoint. What the fuck was I thinking? Why the hell did I ever leave the United States to begin with? And to go to Tijuana of all places? At least risk your American existence for Tulum or Isla Mujeres—but for Avenida Revolucion?! I had not thought this through. I began experiencing shortness of breath. I started to perspire. Maddie noticed I was uncomfortable and asked what was wrong. Quickly running out of options as we approached the immigration checkpoint, and surrounded by my home-boy Eddie and the older Juan, I finally came clean: "I'm illegal."

Maddie looked at me, stunned. This information was a lot to take in, especially given that we were standing at a Border Patrol checkpoint. Eddie told me not to worry. Like he said, they always wave college students through. "And luckily, you can pass for white," Eddie pointed out. Juan, however, who was at this point intoxicated beyond recognition, exclaimed: "Oh, shit." Juan was not helping at all. "Oh, shit," he said louder. When an immigration official looked over at us, Eddie grabbed Juan and took him to another line. Eddie told Maddie and me not to worry—"Keep going without us." We were next up to speak to a United States immigration official. Maddie grabbed my hand and supportively looked me in the eyes. That's when Juan started shouting: "Whatever you do, do not tell 'em you're illegal!"

I almost fainted.

"Next," said the Border Patrol agent.

Maddie pulled me toward that immigration official as we both pretended we didn't know who Juan was.

"Do not tell 'em you're illegal," Juan belligerently continued.

At this point, Eddie also stepped away from Juan, figuring it would be best to pretend not to know the drunk Mexican-looking guy in line. Immigration officials marched up to Juan and told him to please settle down. As opposed to listening to authority, Juan decided to scream: "Rafa! Whatever you do, don't tell 'em you're illegal!"

Juan was escorted out of the line and into some back room, as Maddie and I were waved up to the immigration kiosk. I froze. I didn't know what to do. This was the end of Rafa the Aspiring American. Maddie yanked me toward the Immigration and Customs official, and in front of the whole world to see, she started to kiss me.

Oh.

My.

God.

I mean, if I wasn't going to be allowed back into the country, this was a great way to go out. I finally got my kiss.

The immigration officer was so disgusted by Maddie and my public display of affection that he waved us through: "Go get a room, you two. Next!"

And just like that, I was back on American soil. I could

not believe it. This was incredible! Forget that I managed to get back inside the United States, Maddie had kissed me! Did she secretly harbor feelings for me that she wasn't being honest about? Was she just flirting with those army guys to make me jealous? Did she like me as much as I liked her? I looked at Maddie expectantly. Then she patted me on the shoulder and said, "You're welcome." Maddie started to walk back to the car, but then turned around.

"Don't worry. Your secret's safe with me."

I'm not going to lie. I was a little heartbroken that Maddie didn't see me the same way I saw her. But by God, her kiss got me back into the country, so that was something! Juan, by the way, was detained by Border Patrol that night. He was the American citizen, and I was the unauthorized immigrant. But Juan was darker than I was. He was also highly intoxicated, but don't forget that we were surrounded by an abundance of drunk college kids trying to get back into the country. At the end of the day, my lighter skin got me waved through the immigration checkpoint, and his darker skin got him put in a detention center. My privilege was showing. I was definitely back in the United States.

My idiotic trip to Tijuana made me feel like maybe my immigration issues didn't have to hold me back. Perhaps I could still live a regular, safe American existence. George W. Bush became president at this time and declared in a speech on Mexico relations that: "Scared people build walls, and confident people tear them down." Wow. This president of the United States had some *cojones* to say that out loud for the whole world to hear. Then, September 11 occurred. The Patriot Act was passed. The Department of Homeland Security was created. It was later revealed that the September 11 terrorists had legally entered the United States from Canada. You wouldn't know it by how quickly we militarized the Mexican border. Needless to say, I never went to Tijuana again.

Ma and Pa Kent

I went to see my college counselor once more. Since I had a Mt. SAC ID, I no longer feared talking to administrators. I told my counselor that I was interested in maybe pursuing theater. She pointed out that Mt. SAC did not have the funding for a full theater department, just a much smaller theater program. However, they did have a national championship speech and debate team, which was known as the "forensics" team: "You should consider joining." While the forensics team sounded way too gruesome for me, I told her that I would look into it. In the meantime, I really needed to find a theater department somewhere. After talking to some other theater nerds in my class, I found it in conservative Orange County.

Fullerton College had a pretty impressive theater department. They had a full production house and a complete theater season. They also had an awful lot of talented white kids. I, however, was not there for Shakespeare or any of the musicals they were rehearsing for at the time. I was there for an audition

I read about for an edgy Latino-centric boxing drama the community college was producing written by Oliver Mayer called *Blade to the Heat.* The funny thing about the older white male director of *Blade to the Heat* was that he liked casting incredibly attractive and ridiculously fit young men. I was neither. The fact that I got one of the main roles made me feel good about myself. I figured I had to be talented among all those studs, or else why was I even in this damn show?! I didn't get the lead (a gay boxer struggling with his own sexual identity) and I didn't get the main bad guy (a homophobic boxer not wanting to face the truth about himself). I got the supporting hell-raiser role: an openly bisexual boxer who declared in the middle of the play, "I'll fuck anything—but ain't nobody fucking me!" The character I played was brasher than I would ever be, so I had fun crawling around in his irreverent skin for a change. I asked the director why he cast me, and he said: "It was your smile. You kept smiling throughout the audition, so I knew you could pull off the character." Good to know that I have a bisexual smile. I had no idea.

Blade to the Heat was where I met my lifelong friend and Hollywood partner-in-crime, Steven Garcia. Steven was one of the boxing coordinators for the show. He was a very chiseled, good-looking dude who had no problem being shirtless in the ring. Steven looked like a real-life Clark Kent, whereas I looked like a scrawny, brown Peter Parker standing next to him. I was skinny/fat. That meant that I was on the thinner side, but definitely not in shape. Steven forced me to run a lot of workout drills to get me boxing ready. Steven was a bookish light-skinned Latino from Orange County who grew up on comic books and skateboarding. He used to be an overweight little kid who loved movies and was really close to his mom. If that wasn't enough like my own story, Steven also considered his stepdad to be his real dad. More remarkable still was that he preferred Sprite over Coke—and ginger ale over both! But let me tell you, there's nothing worse than meeting someone who is exactly like you, but is a better-looking version of you. Steven was so much like me that I even wondered if he had immigration problems.

Outside of expanding my inner circle with comic book nerds, there's one other important thing you need to know about the *Blade to the Heat* performance. Yes, my family sold out another opening weekend. And yes, I was nominated for Best Actor by the Kennedy Center American College Theater Festival (more on this in a moment). But the only thing that mattered to me about the *Blade to the Heat* performance was that Liesel and Steve showed up. Now, you're probably wondering, *Who the hell are Liesel and Steve?* Allow me to introduce you to my American parents…

When my counselor told me Mt. SAC had a national championship speech and debate team, I didn't want to do it at first. But the notion of "national" stuck with me. I couldn't travel abroad because of my immigration status, but that didn't mean I couldn't go *national*. The idea of doing anything outside the San Gabriel Valley excited me. I cautiously attended the introductory forensics team meeting and was surprised to see a ragtag group of outcasts. There were other Latinos,

Black folk, LGBTQ+, AAPI, disabled students—it was a multicultural wonderland! The forensics team quickly felt like home because they were all nerdy and artsy like me. I wasn't interested in giving speeches, but I did feel very comfortable being around minorities eager to express themselves.

The forensics team head coach, Liesel Reinhart, was a force to be reckoned with. She was young, she was white (her last name was Reinhart, for crying out loud!), and she commanded a room unlike anyone I had ever seen before. If she didn't have such high morals, Liesel would have been a US senator. Her unwavering confidence might have come from all her years of doing speech and debate, but it actually came from the fact that she was the winningest collegiate speech coach in the United States. If forensics was the NBA, Liesel was Phil Jackson.

Liesel's life partner, Steven T. Seagle, was not an official coach, but he showed up to help the team whenever there was practice. Liesel and Steve met doing forensics in college, but at this point in his life he was simply looking to spend more quality time with the very busy Liesel. Steve literally volunteered as a speech coach just so he could see Liesel for dinner. You sure as hell didn't become Phil Jackson by going home early! I took a fast liking to the sarcastic Steve, a tall, skinny white guy with a voice deeper than Vin Diesel's. Or maybe he took a fast liking to me, which was why he let me into his orbit so quickly. Steve was a very busy Hollywood writer. He never alienated anybody, but he could take on only a few students at a time to coach. Again, he wasn't being paid for any of this.

Half a semester into the class, I was in the forensics room one evening helping Steve build a set for a speech performance when Liesel popped her head in and informed me that Steve was also a comic book writer. I freaked out. I was an avid comic book reader, and Liesel knew that. I had so many questions.

"Have you written any comics I know?" I asked.

"That depends," Steve answered, "on what comics you know."

Without knowing what comics he had written, I went straight into asking Steve about hypothetical fights between superheroes we would never see due to trademark violations.

"Who would win, Batman or Wolverine?"

"Wolverine."

"Wolverine or Superman?"

"Superman."

"What about Superman or Spider-Man?"

"Still Superman."

"Okay, but what about Superman or the Hulk?"

"It's always going to be Superman, Rafa. It's in his name. You get it—truth, justice, the American way."

That night at home, I thought a lot about Superman. Superman was not a character I ever liked much. I liked Christopher Reeve in the original film; I thought he was great. But the character? I have pictures of myself dressed as Batman as a child. I even have one of me dressed up as the little-remembered Greatest American Hero. But Superman? He felt so bland. He was like an overgrown Boy Scout in red underwear. But it was what Steve had said that stuck with me: "truth, justice, the American way." As I lay in bed with my eyes open, it dawned on me that the most interesting thing about Superman was not his superpowers at all, but that he was secretly not American. Here was an alien trying to fit in the best he could in his newly adopted country. He loved the United States so much that he fought for its values: truth, justice, and the American way. He was basically fighting for life, liberty, and the pursuit of happiness. But nobody could ever know that Clark Kent was also Superman. It would put all his loved ones in great peril if the truth ever came out.

Thanks to Steve, I started seeing so much of myself in the Kryptonian American. Superman—above all superheroes—was the perfect example of what a migrant child could accomplish in the United States when shown the proper love and support by the American community. I had been a Superman all this time, but I didn't realize it because I lived in such fear of anybody learning my secret identity.

I looked through my comic book collection to see if I had any Superman comics. That's when I came across *Uncanny X-Men*, issue 350. It was one of my favorite X-Men stories of all time: Gambit's greatest secret revealed! It was an issue of great importance for the Marvel company. And there in front of my face was the writer's name: "Steven T. Seagle." My Steve. Wow. He had been affecting my life since before I had ever met him. As for him and Liesel being my American parents, more on that in a second.

The secrets I kept were usually between my family and me versus the rest of the world. But there was one secret I even kept from my parents: I wanted to major in theater. Up to this point, they figured it was just a hobby. But since my immigration limbo kept me confined to community college indefinitely, I had the time to discover in college what I really wanted to do in life. And storytelling—any form of it—was it for me. So for as bad as my not being able to transfer out of community college was, my immigration problems truly led me to my career in the entertainment industry. Looking back, I probably loved theater because I needed the attention. Perhaps the love and admiration from their community is all an undocumented student ever really needs.

There was nothing like coming out of the dressing room to your family after a long, exhausting physical performance— especially one that contained a lot of boxing choreography like *Blade to the Heat*. But after opening week, my family stopped coming. Fullerton was very far for everyone. Besides, they had already seen the show, so I had no reason to go out after the performance. I didn't know anybody in Orange County except Steven Garcia, who was in the show with me. So I would just stay in my dressing room most nights. One evening, toward the end of the run, someone from the crew walked over and told me I had family waiting outside. *Family?* Surprised, I ran out to see who had come back. I was shocked to discover Liesel and Steve waiting for me. I don't remember inviting them, but they were there nonetheless. The crew member was right—I did have *family* outside.

As much as I loved theater, I loved Liesel and Steve more. For someone who was always looking for acceptance and security wherever I went because I was always waiting for the other shoe to drop, I finally found it with Steve and Liesel. I made the decision to stop pursuing theater for a while and fully concentrated on forensics. What can I say? Showing up is one of my love languages.

We took a writer's retreat to Big Bear Lake as a team to prepare our new speeches for competition. I had never done anything as luxurious as taking time off just to concentrate on writing. This was wonderful. A getaway to be creative. It was as if they were talking dirty to me!

I was asked to join the Speech to Entertain category. This was Liesel and Steve's specialty. Steve's dry wit and Liesel's show-stopping one-liners were a deadly combination. I loved bouncing ideas off them. It was fun, but it was also grueling. You really had to be sharp to hold your own with those two. This would technically be my first exposure to what a professional TV writers' room would feel like, minus all the imposter syndrome!

I found my voice as a writer doing forensics. I wrote a comedic speech about our broken immigration system. Young writers should always start with what they know. Funny enough, I didn't know much about how our immigration system actually worked. In researching the topic, I discovered that "illegal" was the worst possible word to use when describing undocumented immigrants. People can't be illegal; only actions can. If you believe human beings can be illegal, then I beg you to think of this: When a person kills another person, they are not an *illegal*—they are a murderer. When a person steals something from another person, they are not an *illegal*—they are a thief. When a person forgets to rinse before putting the dishes into the washer, they are not an *illegal*—they just forgot this one time, Mom! So why would we call a group of people in search of a better life, working on the front lines, essential workers during a global pandemic, yearning to breathe free "illegals"? If that wasn't enough, I also discovered that the word "illegal" was designed to criminalize a section of our population specifically to try to deny them their First Amendment right to free speech and their First Amendment right to assemble. Needless to say, I was having a political awakening. I even came to realize that my previous lack of political awareness was a political statement unto itself.

I loved doing forensics. With my Mt. SAC ID, I was able to get on planes and travel to obscure cities across America, like Walla Walla, Washington, on the weekends to compete in empty classrooms in preliminary rounds and in packed auditoriums for the out rounds. And for me, it was all about those packed auditoriums. Liesel and Steve were the perfect writing mentors: Liesel would help me with substance, while Steve helped me with structure and my comedic voice. My first year, the majority minority forensics team and I destroyed the national community college competition. We were so good that Liesel had secretly decided to take a select few students to an international speech and debate tournament in Prague.

Liesel called me into her office to tell me the good news. With a smile she reserved only when changing students' lives, she said: "We have decided to take you to Prague." My heart sank. I knew the international trip might be a possibility for me, but I never actually thought I would be selected. And worse, I never thought I'd have to turn it down in person. Couldn't Liesel have just sent me a letter in the mail like all those other universities trying to ask me for my social security number? I was undocumented. I couldn't go to Prague. Or more clearly, I could go to Prague but then I wouldn't be allowed back into the country. I broke eye contact with Liesel—a major forensics no-no—and said that I couldn't go. I started sputtering excuses, saying I was busy that month. I should have known Liesel wouldn't leave it alone. The reason speech and debate is called "forensics" is because the word is defined as the search for truth, which is what we do in a debate. And nobody embodies that sentiment better than Liesel herself. She always needed to get to the bottom of any matter.

"Why can't you go? That's ridiculous. Do you know how many students would die for a free trip to Prague?"

I looked up at Liesel, unsure of what to say. Up to this point, only my family, close high school friends, and my few *Rooster* cast mates knew the truth about my immigration status. Maddie was the only person who was not Latina who knew, but she was cast as a Latina. She was also my age. Liesel was older than me and an authority figure. But Liesel was also somebody who never meant anyone any harm and always went out of her way to support me. She drove an hour and a half to watch my performance of *Blade to the Heat* for me! We had become close. I didn't know what to say. I was utterly confused. I was also very exhausted from all the lying, and goddamn it, I really wanted to go to Prague! I looked at my new mentor and finally said, "I can't go because I'm illegal." (I know I just learned to use "undocumented," but old habits die hard!)

Liesel was the first white person in a position of power that I ever told about my immigration status. It was a very frightening experience. I didn't know it then, but her reaction had a great effect on my young adult life. She could have been troubled by the news, or offended by my unauthorized status. A simple disgusted gesture would have made me feel great shame. Instead, like she would time and again in my life, Liesel leaned in and assured me everything would be okay. She first made sure that I was calm and felt safe. Then she was inquisitive like only Liesel could be. "How is that possible? When did you come here? Did you try hiring an immigration lawyer?" But no matter how much I explained the details of my immigration problems, she couldn't quite understand how I could still be "illegal." Without letting me leave her office, Liesel called counselors, the vice president of Student Services, and other administrators. She didn't mention my name, but she perfectly described the predicament I was in. But nothing. There was not a thing she or anybody else could do to help me. I already knew that, but still it filled my heart to watch her try.

The forensics team went on to Prague without me. Steve sent me a picture of my face superimposed on the group photo. I thought that was very sweet. I brought home the movie *Superman* from work one night. The old 1978 Christopher Reeve version. A young farm boy who grows up to be one of America's greatest heroes...and all he needed was a secret identity and two loving adoptive American parents.

How to Disappoint Your Immigrant Parents without Trying

My mom was a doctor and my dad was a doctor, so I officially decided to major in theater. I'll admit it was a dumb decision to get a degree in something that wouldn't make me money right away. As an immigrant, how the hell was I going to take care of my mom and dad with a theater degree? I was a child whose parents sacrificed their livelihoods and medical careers so that I could have a shot at a better life, and I let everything ride on the arts! I even applied to UCLA's School of Theater, Film & Television. The question of my real social security number came up again, and it was wearing on me. Paperwork is terrible under normal, documented circumstances. Now compound that with the fear of having your entire life uprooted and erased by just filling out a form. I can't even go to restaurants that ask you to fill out your own order—it triggers me!

Over dinner one evening, my dad said he saw that I was applying to universities.

"What major did you choose?"

I tensed up. Things were getting better between us, but he never really probed too much about college. With the most stoic face possible, I replied: "Theater." As I had imagined, I disappointed my dad to no end. I felt guilty because they had sacrificed so much for my sake and still I chose the most unstable path. Yes, he liked my performances, but he never thought I would pursue this acting thing as a career. By the way, my backup major, world religions, was even more devastating to him. Because what billionaire in America has not mastered the art of theater and the beliefs of every major world religion?

My dad asked, "Are you sure this is what you want to do?"

"I am sure," I answered defiantly.

My dad looked over at my mom with great concern, but she simply responded with an it's-his-life shoulder shrug. There was so much my dad wanted to say, but he bit his tongue. Worried and quite frustrated, there wasn't much he *could* say that would have any bearing on my ultimate decision. He told me to pay for my own schooling when I first got to college, and I did; thus, I had complete autonomy over my higher education. Even though we had no documentation, I still found a way to have a full-time job, be a full-time student, and do theater and speech on my off time. I knew my dad was upset about my career choice, but I didn't care. I had to live my best unauthorized-life.

Shortly thereafter, I was summoned into the office of Mt. SAC theater professor Ralph Eastman. A tall, classy white man with a love for folk music, Professor Eastman informed me that I had been nominated to attend the Kennedy Center American College Theater Festival Regional Acting Competition.

"This is a big deal for Mt. SAC," Professor Eastman said. "If you manage to win regionals, you'd be only the second student to make it to the national competition in our college's history."

It was on! I needed to make it to nationals. My dad thought my career choice was a travesty, but the universe was trying to help me prove him wrong. All I had to do was beat a thousand other students and make it to the national competition.

Soon thereafter, I learned that I was nominated at not one but two of the community colleges I attended: for my work in both Mt. SAC's *Roosters* and Fullerton College's *Blade to the Heat*. Both colleges had to go into arbitration over who would take credit for me. I'm certain this type of nomination must have meant more fund-raising dollars for each of them. Mt. SAC, since they were the first official nomination, ended up winning in the end.

I was heading to the competition representing Mt. SAC, but I still needed two pieces of material for this competition: a monologue and a scene, which required an acting partner. The acting partner was easy. There was no doubt I was going to beg my homeboy Eddie, the cholo Shakespeare aficionado who had gone to Nogales High School, to be my scene partner. It was almost serendipitous since Nogales High School was the school my parents didn't allow me to attend in fear I would turn into a gangbanger. I would have been a terrible gang member, reciting soliloquies in my oversize khakis and hairnet all the time. Eddie and I started working on a scene from an obscure play called *Cuba & His Teddy Bear* by Reinaldo Povod. The play was an explosive drama about a small-town drug dealer and his son. I played the drug dealer and Eddie played my son. Because the scene was heavy, I knew my monologue needed to be light and comedic. Luckily, Kenny Klawiter was both hilarious and a huge theater savant. Kenny ran the Mt. SAC speech and debate team with Liesel. A gorgeous man with Midwestern charm, Kenny was the type of communications professor who would get gifts at the end of each semester from his admiring female students. Unfortunately for all his brides-in-waiting, Kenny was a proud gay man. Speaking of which, Kenny also taught me one of the most valuable lessons in life when it came to prejudging others. We once drove to a forensics tournament together, and out of curiosity I asked him, "When did you first know you were gay?" Kenny smiled at me kindly and replied, "When did you first know you were straight?" *Damn.* I never realized that oppressed people could oppress people.

I was in Kenny's office telling him I was in desperate need of a funny monologue, and I felt it needed to be ethnic. I was entering a big regional acting competition going up against roughly a thousand college students. My ethnicity needed to be my superpower. "I think I have the right play for you," Kenny said with a glint of mischievousness in his eyes. Kenny was a theater nerd just like I was, so he had a wealth of knowledge when it came to modern plays. He reached behind his chair to a giant bookshelf and handed me the monologue that would define my regional acting competition. It was called *Men on the Verge of a His-Panic Breakdown* by Guillermo Reyes. The play was erratic and irreverent. More important, it was a one-person show written by a Latino. It was a series of glorious comedic monologues, and the one I chose to perform was that of a gay immigrant who arrives in Los Angeles during the 1992 uprisings and becomes convinced he's witnessing the filming of another *Lethal Weapon* sequel. It was perfect. I had my scene, my scene partner, and my monologue. *Fresno, here I come.*

The Western Conference Regional Acting Competition that year was held in Fresno, California. Negatively referred to as the armpit of the state, I found Fresno to be quite lovely. It had a lot of land and a lot of great people. My people. Fresno wasn't very glamorous, but it was close enough for me to drive. I was a safe driver. The only time I had ever been pulled over was the Free Rafa incident where the cop really pulled Choli over, not me. There was nothing my parents could do about me driving to Fresno. My older cousin Priscilla was getting rid of her car, and her dad, my uncle Sergio, suggested she give it to me. And that is how I came to possess the *chalupa*, a hard-on-the-outside-but-soft-on-the-inside beat-up white Toyota Camry. The caveat was that I was only allowed to drive the chalupa to and from school. Since the Kennedy Center American College Theater Festival Regional Acting Competition was school-related, I figured driving to Fresno from West Covina was fair game. It was a loophole, but fair game nonetheless.

The drive to Fresno was a little scary. It was just my homeboy Eddie and me. We could have been pulled over at any time and my collegiate acting aspirations—let alone my American citizenship aspirations—would have been over. Eddie knew the truth about my immigration status because of our little Tijuana trip, but he didn't seem to care much. We were just excited to have an excuse to get away from our neighborhood.

Eddie and I arrived in Fresno, and as we checked into our motel, we realized that everyone was there to party. The lobby was loud, and the pool, which all the students were drinking in, was even louder. I was even offered to be part of a three-some. I was so young and inexperienced that I simply said, "I can't—I don't have call waiting."

University, Cal State, and community college students separated from their parents for the first time are always eager to wild out. I wasn't. As you know, I had been drinking from an early age, but I was there for one thing and one thing only: to win the acting competition and prove to my parents that I was not stupid for wanting to do this as a career.

Like speech and debate, there were a lot of preliminary rounds in the ballrooms before you could get to the out rounds in the big auditorium for the semifinals. And if you were lucky, you got to perform on the main stage of the Tower

Theatre for the Performing Arts for the entire region in the finals. I rehearsed my monologue alone at night in my motel room, and Eddie and I rehearsed our scene in the mornings. The days were full of cutthroat competitive rounds. Everyone was really good—the four-year students most of all. They were very polished, unlike us scrappy two-year students. The competition lasted several days. I was laser-focused. I had convinced myself that I could prove my dad wrong on my career choice with this win. I was so intent on winning the competition that Eddie claims the following happened (but I have no recollection)...

I begrudgingly agreed to go with Eddie to one of the many competition socials they held around town. Everyone was drinking, dancing, and having the time of their lives. I, on the other hand, was counting the minutes before I could go run my monologue back in my motel room again. In the middle of the dance floor—for everyone to hear—a beautiful young lady yelled out, "I want to *%$# him!" Eddie claims she pointed at me. I didn't hear this because I was running my lines in my head the whole time. Do I remember the social? Barely. Do I remember this young lady? Not really. Did I hear someone yell out, "I want to *%$# him!" Definitely not. I'm very happy this young lady had the confidence and self-assurance to yell something out like that for the whole region to hear. I'm also happy this young lady and I didn't *%$# because I would have just been running my monologue in my head for the full two-and-a-half minutes. I continued walking, and Eddie was stunned that I didn't go talk to her.

Eddie and I made it out of prelims, we made it out of quarterfinals to semifinals, and we miraculously made the list for the final round. We were beside ourselves, in large part because the competition was open to all community college students, but it was mostly dominated by theater students from four-year universities. They were the big men and women on campus, always walking around with their heads held high and an air of invincibility around them. It was a big deal for Eddie and me to make the finals. It was an even bigger deal for Mt. SAC, which was not really known for their performing arts—just their cross-country course. The final round would have been nerve-racking for me, except that I had done a lot of speech and debate up to that point. I felt comfortable in front of a large audience. I knew exactly if and when I had their undivided attention. I didn't need a spotlight to wash away the public. I felt at home looking people in the eye. Plus, I had my homeboy Eddie by my side.

I took the center stage of the Tower Theatre and introduced myself. I rolled my R in "Rrrrrrrafael" for the whole Western United States to hear. I went straight into my monologue and the laughter that came back at me from the packed, standing room–only performing arts center felt like a tidal wave. It is an experience nobody can ever prepare you for. You have to be able to ride the wave and not get lost in the laughter. That's what makes elite stand-ups so great: the ability to ride that wave. I did my best to manage the audience's cackles and then transitioned into my dramatic scene. Eddie joined me onstage. At that point, it was no longer a competition. It was just two boys from a historically rough neighborhood doing what they loved.

At the awards breakfast the next day, we were all aware that only two people—two teams, more precisely—would go on to the national competition at the Kennedy Center in Washington, DC, to represent our region. The region was made up of five states. That was who the two winners would be representing. If you were into emerging theater artists, this was a gigantic deal. The first winner was announced and there was a polite clap. He was an older white college student with perfect Jesus of Nazareth hair. He was from Cal State Fullerton. I remembered him doing a very cool Shakespearean monologue that nobody could understand—because who the *%$# still spoke Shakespearean? The dude went up to the front to receive his award in a very diplomatic manner, as if he already knew he was getting a giant promotion at work. He went up alone without his scene partner. I guess that made sense since he was the official nominee and not the scene partner. Then they announced the second winner. This, too, was a bit of a blur for me, like the young lady declaring her affection at the party in the middle of the dance floor. All I remember is Eddie and me both jumping on our chairs. We weren't supposed to win, but we did. We weren't supposed to jump on our chairs, but we also did. Eddie and I ran around the banquet room high-fiving everyone. Our excitement was contagious. Even the cranky tournament directors couldn't help but laugh. Eddie and I screamed, did a victory dance, and bear-hugged the uncomfortable male announcer. Holy shit. The Latino boys from San Gabriel Valley won. I couldn't wait to tell my dad.

In the chalupa on the way back to West Covina from Fresno, Eddie and I were still in shock. Eddie eventually looked at me and said, "We came to win this thing...and we did." Eddie paused, taking in the Central California landscape. He then thanked me for choosing him as my partner. Eddie was like a lot of my homeboys in my area—vastly talented (more talented than me!), but always went unseen and ignored by non-Hispanics. But I saw Eddie in his baggy clothes and shaved head, and hoped that he thought I was cool enough to hang around with. Luckily, he did. And on top of that, he helped me perfect my first role onstage. Lost in my thoughts, I swerved. As the adrenaline from the win started to wear off, I suddenly remembered that I was an undocumented immigrant driving a car with no license. I wondered if the highway patrol would care that I was about to represent our entire state at a national acting competition.

I got home and told my parents what had transpired. My mom screamed in excitement. My dad just nodded his head. As always, they were bewildered by the things I did. I had just won a five-state acting competition and was now being flown to Washington, DC, to compete for a national title. My dad continued to look at me. He was clearly thinking about something, but he didn't say anything. Maybe he felt he didn't want to kill the moment.

I wasn't worried about flying because I was told my school ID would suffice. My mom was a little worried, but I knew it would be fine. I was being chaperoned by Professor East-man, after all. When Eddie and I arrived at the airport for the national competition, Eddie was stunned to discover that we weren't going to Washington State.

"We're going to Washington, DC," he exclaimed. "What the fuck? I didn't pack for the East Coast."

Until Eddie said that, it didn't hit me that we were going to our nation's capital. I, too, thought we were going to Washington State. But I didn't let Eddie know that. Instead, I made fun of him for being so dumb. "Washington State...stuuuupid."

I had never been to Washington, DC. I had no idea what the *DC* even stood for! *Diverse Colony?* And now I was asked to perform at the Kennedy Center a few blocks from Homeland Security. The nerves started to kick in, but they had nothing to do with the performance.

Like the regional competition, there were a lot of events at the Kennedy Center during the week. But I wasn't there for any of that. I got this far, and by God, I was determined to win, if just to continue to prove to my dad that I had chosen the right path. I also wanted to do it quickly before anyone discovered I was not supposed to be in the city, let alone the country. That was when I got the biggest surprise of my life. Walking back into our DC hotel after a long day of theater workshops, I discovered two people in the lobby that I never expected to see in our country's capital—my mom and dad. My eyes welled up with tears from the shock. My parents had arrived in Washington, DC, to support me—me and my crazy pipe dream of working in theater. That was what my dad had been deciding when I first got back from Fresno, but didn't want to say. He wondered if he and my mom should risk coming to Washington, DC, or not. To know what that decision meant to me, you have to understand that my parents had never flown on a plane since we'd arrived in the United States out of fear that they might be detained. My parents had also never taken a vacation in the fourteen years that we had been in this country because—like so many other immigrants before them—they, too, were slaves to the minimum wage. They worked every day. Nonstop. But they finally stopped working for a few days... for me.

When the night came and I finally took center stage at the Kennedy Center, nothing that I had been holding against my dad mattered anymore. Nor did I care about the venue, the audience, or even the win. I performed that night for the only two people in the world who mattered to me. I performed for the reason I was in this country to begin with. The bright spotlight made it impossible to see any of the audience members from the large stage, but I saw my mom and dad clearly, proudly smiling up at me from the front row. Three undocumented immigrants taking up space in our nation's capital.

Out of all the college students performing that evening, I was one of three who were from a community college, one of two who were Latino, and the only one who was undocumented that I know of. I didn't win the national competition. Some random dude doing Shakespeare did. If I learned anything from this experience is that Shakespeare always fuckin' wins! But my real victory was having my parents find their strength to set foot in this nation's capital. It wasn't easy for them. It took them fourteen years and a really good reason to do so.

Before we left, my parents and I walked to the Lincoln Memorial and I looked up at the Great Emancipator who tried to end the institution of slavery and was assassinated for it. He was gunned down for America's original sin. I looked up at President Lincoln, made up mostly of Georgian marble, and wondered what he would have thought of us as immigrants. It turns out, one of President Lincoln's signature pieces of legislation, the Act to Encourage Immigration, signed on July 4, 1864, was the first and last law in American history to ever encourage immigration to the United States. It was repealed soon after his assassination.

My parents and I arrived at our condo in West Covina shortly after landing at LAX. At the doorway, my dad asked me a very simple question: "What now?" I didn't know how to respond. I didn't know what now. I was maxed out on my college credits, and I had taken this college acting thing as far as I could—literally to the front steps of the United States Capitol. Like I did after high school, I simply responded with: "I'll figure it out." My mom returned from the mailbox holding two large envelopes. They were both for me. I opened the first one and discovered my acceptance to UCLA. My eyes started to well up. The University of California, Los Angeles, wanted me. I opened the second envelope and found our acceptance for our permanent residency requests from the United States of America. After fourteen years we were finally . . . legal. My parents and I hugged each other. Tears started running down our faces. The moment felt too unbelievable to be true. They finally found the vindication they had been waiting for—their monumental sacrifice to come to this country had finally paid off. We continued to hold each other as we collapsed on the cold tile floor. At this point, all we could do was cry.

Affirmative Action
Cookie Sale

My parents and I nervously sat inside a large, gray federal building in downtown Los Angeles. We were there for our collective permanent residencies interview. The plastic blue chairs we were sitting on were meant to add some color to the monotone space. A portrait of a mischievously smiling George W. Bush hung on the wall. My mom and dad kept looking at my T-shirt disapprovingly. I had bought it at a Rage Against the Machine concert and emblazoned across it was a blue upside-down triangle, a purposeful reminder of what the Nazis made the Jews wear in concentration camps. The triangle in this instance was worn by foreign forced laborers and immigrants. I was proud to be making a political statement inside a federal building. My parents, however, wanted to find a rock to crawl under. Oh, did I mention that the T-shirt also had the word "ILLEGAL" spelled out inside the blue upside-down triangle?

That's right: my parents sat next to their son wearing a T-shirt that said "ILLEGAL," as they waited to speak to the United States immigration authorities. It was the spring of 2001.

After waiting for nearly an hour and a half, an African American man of great physical stature called us into his office. As was always the case when we were with English-speaking people of authority, I did most of the talking. The federal worker looked at my T-shirt and chuckled. My parents felt more at ease knowing that a representative of our potential new country got my sense of humor. My dad slid our folders across the man's desk. They contained all our records and documentation while in this country. The federal immigration employee looked through every page. He noticed that my folder was filled with elementary school Student of the Month awards, high school honor roll certificates, my first communion certificate, my community college speech national championship title, my regional acting award, one LA County recognition for my volunteer work, and my acceptance letter to UCLA. He stopped at the acceptance letter and carefully reviewed it. His eyes met mine, and the man said: "We're going to have to speed up this process to make sure you get to UCLA." He smiled, knowing too well that he was changing my life for the better. But that was when things got a little complicated.

We were almost "legal," but first we had to take a series of health tests to make sure we didn't have any illnesses. I had no idea that one of those tests would be an STD test. I was freakin' out because I had been recently sexually active, and—

worse—I had not used a condom. Very stupid of me! The two weeks we had to wait for our STD results were the two longest, most excruciating, painful weeks of my life. My unprotected sex was about to ruin my family's chances of becoming permanent residents of the United States. My teenage rite of passage was driving me into a neurotic spiral. I hated myself and my teenage hormones. I wished I could deport my penis. I promised God that I would never have sex again, as long as she (my God is a chola God, by the way) allowed us to become permanent residents of this country. If this wasn't bad enough, my parents also insisted on picking up our STD results together at the doctor's office. Could this entire experience get any more awkward?!

We were handed our results by the nurse simultaneously and time...simply...slowed...down. Everything moved in slow motion. My vision got a little blurry. I finally got my eyes to focus on my test results, and sure enough, I was negative. What an incredible relief. I had never felt so positive for being so negative! Now clear to become a permanent resident, I quickly made an addendum to my agreement with God: I would never have *unprotected* sex again.

Because of my lack of chlamydia and gonorrhea, our green cards arrived in the mail several months after our STD tests. My parents and I were finally permanent residents of the United States of America. It was remarkable to think that over time I would no longer be afraid to: travel, be questioned by the police, fill out a job application, drive a car, go into a federal building, enter a hospital, get a credit card, or go to a public school. I wasn't having sex anymore, but I made a bunch of appointments at the county's free STD clinic simply because I could!

The University of California, Los Angeles, is one of the most beautiful campuses I've ever set foot on. The most important figures of the past century—from Albert Einstein to Martin Luther King Jr.—all spoke at UCLA. Two of the greatest American athletes of the past hundred years—Jackie Robinson and Kareem Abdul-Jabbar—attended UCLA. Angela Davis and Judy Baca both taught there; James Dean and Jim Morrison took classes there. But more important, my dad always dreamed of working there—at UCLA Medical. Since he couldn't reach that dream for himself, I figured that maybe I could do it for him.

I was summoned to meet with a Latino group on campus before the start of the school year. I'm pretty sure I was up for a scholarship. I sat across from three Latino college students, one guy and two girls. They were curious about my personal essay, which I'd titled "The Wetback." The essay seemed to raise some concerns for the committee. I told them that a few years back, I discovered that I didn't have papers, and that I hated how this derogatory term was used on people like me. The conversation was going well until one of the Latinas asked, "What are your thoughts on affirmative action?" *Oh, interesting.* I had never reflected much on the topic before, outside of when my high school counselor told me I was in a great position to benefit from it. But then I attended Mt. SAC and heard an older white philosophy professor say that affirmative action was flawed because two wrongs don't make a right. I didn't really know what either of them meant, but not knowing what else to say, I simply reiterated what my male philosophy professor said because it sounded provocative.

"Two wrongs don't make a right," I said, and grinned, proud of being so quick on my feet.

The problem with plagiarizing other people's thoughts is that you don't have their follow-up remarks ready to go. The committee looked at each other, concerned, and then continued:

"How so?" the Latina asked me curiously.

"Oh, I don't know. They just, kinda, don't."

"But you obviously have an opinion on the matter," chimed in the Latino student. "Please elaborate."

I had nothing left to say. The committee let out a collective sigh. I could tell that they were cheering for me, but that I wasn't helping my own cause. I was caught red-handed pretending to be smarter than I was. Looking back, I must have sounded stupid to a group of community-focused students trying to help incoming transfers from marginalized communities achieve at UCLA. But it wasn't my fault. I had been taught by predominantly white professors my whole life, and not all could be as progressive as Liesel and Steve. My sensibilities were mostly that of white Americans. I loved Shania Twain and Kelsey Grammer. The problem was that nobody taught me in high school that affirmative action didn't start with the Civil Rights Movement of the 1960s. Affirmative action has existed since the founding of this nation. It's just that for the first hundred and eighty-five years of America, it benefited those who were white and male: only white males could own property; only white males could vote; only white males could travel freely. Once affirmative action started to benefit people outside that group, the practice needed to be stopped immediately for some unknown reason. (Come on, you know the damn reason!) If I was going to plagiarize anybody, I should have plagiarized Chris Rock when he said, "I don't think I should get accepted into a school over a white person if I get a lower mark. But if there's a tie, fuck 'em. Shit, you had a four-hundred-year head start, mothafucker." But don't quote me on that. Needless to say, I never heard from that student committee again.

UCLA professor Jose Luis Valenzuela was the first Latino educator I ever had in my entire higher education career. Can you imagine? I went throughout my entire scholastic journey in Southern California before running into somebody at the college level who shared my immigrant experience in this country.

Our lives collided in a very Latino way. I had been commuting to UCLA from West Covina for my classes. I would leave my house every day at 5:30 a.m. with my mom so she could drop me off at the train station before work. I would then take the Metrolink from Covina into Union Station in downtown LA, catch the subway (the Red Line) up to Wilshire and Western, and then jump on a Metro bus that headed to UCLA so I could make my 8:00 a.m. class with five minutes to spare. This commute was precise. Nothing could go wrong. And if my mom ever had an early morning shift, I would get to UCLA before the buildings even opened. On those days, I was fortunate enough that the Spanish-speaking janitorial staff would let me into the building and allow me to sleep on the couch before they officially opened the school.

One particular fall morning, I got to UCLA so early that I even beat the janitorial staff to work. I was so exhausted from my commute that I fell asleep on a bench outside the theater building. I woke up when I felt a presence standing over me. It was Jose Luis, looking down at me with his rugged white beard. He didn't know who I was, yet he said: "I don't want anybody to see you sleeping out here on the bench." Translation: I don't want anybody to see a Latino student sleeping out here on the bench. Without knowing me, Jose Luis handed me his spare key and said: "If you ever get to school this early again, please go to my office and sleep there." And just as quickly, Jose Luis was gone. I was shocked. Jose Luis didn't know who I was, but I knew who he was. Every student did. He had a no BS aura about him. All the directing students always worked their hardest to impress Jose Luis. He was an intimidating presence to most students. Not to me. He just looked like my uncle! With that simple act of kindness, Jose Luis handed me the key to his kingdom—both literally and figuratively.

I left the bench and walked straight into Jose Luis's office. His tiny work space was a goddamn disaster. He was a mad artistic genius and his office looked like a mad artistic genius's studio. Because of my dad, I was a neat freak. Remember, my dad was a pediatric surgeon and the emergency room needed to be perfectly clean at all times for the sake of the patient's life. My room was always as clean as an ICU. There was no way I could sleep inside Jose Luis's office. The mess gave me anxiety. I started to clean up the place, not for him, but for me. I wasn't going to be caught dead in a dump like this. When Jose Luis returned later that day, he was so impressed by how well I had organized and coordinated his paperwork (i.e., mess) that he made me his teacher's assistant while I was still an undergrad. I'm sure we broke some rules doing this, but Jose Luis and I were people who always existed in the margins. For us, rules were meant to be broken. Or in my case, cleaned up very nicely, organized alphabetically, and then broken.

In all my years of schooling, I may have had one or two US-born Latino teachers before Jose Luis, but they all shared my "general market" sensibilities. Jose Luis was an immigrant and proud of it. Jose Luis was part of the Chicano theater movement, which was ignited by Luis Valdez and the work he did with Cesar Chavez to support the farmworkers of Delano. Jose Luis was a well-respected theater director in Los Angeles and always carried a lot of gravitas and respect with him around campus. Jose Luis was so freakin' Latino that he was the artistic director of the Latino Theater Company. He was the mentor I had been longing for my whole life.

One morning, I found myself walking through the south side of the UCLA campus. I rarely made it out that far south.

UCLA was big, but it was very segregated. I was always on the north side of campus with all the free liberal arts folks. The south side was where all the students were enslaved to their majors: math, engineering, computer science, and other nerdy stuff that promised to make you millions. As I was walking, I suddenly heard a commotion nearby. A bunch of students were arguing around a table where two Campus Republicans had mounted a sign that announced "Affirmative Action Cookie Sale." The multicultural students encircling the table were not happy, but the two white frat guys behind the table were very pleased with themselves. They were trying to teach the entire student body a lesson on the evils of affirmative action by selling cookies to white students for five dollars, but to minority students for fifty cents. People were upset. The students of color did not want their damn cookies. Well, I'm sure a few did because it was a great deal, but nobody ever caved.

I auditioned for all the UCLA school plays but didn't get cast in anything. I auditioned for Shakespeare, Tennessee Williams, Arthur Miller, and a bunch of other dead white dudes—but nothing. I knew the theater department at UCLA was harder to get into than Harvard Law, but this was ridiculous. I considered changing my major to sociology or something even more vague. Then somebody decided to mount a student production of *Short Eyes* by Miguel Piñero, which is a prison drama, and I got the lead role. I was ecstatic. I was finally going to perform on a UCLA stage. But in the middle of rehearsal one evening with the predominantly Black and brown cast, I thought: *Hold up, I can't be in Victorian England but I can be in Sing Sing!* I was furious. But *Short Eyes* was actually directed by a talented young Black woman, Noni, who, like me, was also a Jose Luis Valenzuela protégée. So the problem was more complicated than people only being able to see me as a criminal. The problem was that unless the role was ethno-specific, directors at UCLA would not think to cast a person of color. I know this because Jose Luis was part of a faculty committee trying to address this very issue: student directors not casting minority student actors in their productions. Their responses to the problem were naive, sincere, and quite remarkably heartbreaking: "It's not that we don't want to cast minorities—it's just that when we read a script, we think of Brad Pitt and Leonardo DiCaprio so we cast accordingly." This was not Hollywood. This was an institution of higher learning, and already the faculty had their hands full trying to combat internalized white supremacy caused by the entertainment industry. It was exhausting being a student from a marginalized community at UCLA. I couldn't wait to see what the real world had in store for me. Yay.

A few weeks later it was revealed that the Affirmative Action Cookie Sale was not something the Campus Republicans had come up with on their own. It was actually a right-wing radio host who had reached out to the student group and fully funded the stunt, which ended up garnering a lot of local media attention. This was done at the height of Rush Limbaugh: a right-wing personality who was successful at conflating racism and sexism with individual patriotism. As I came to learn, this was a common theme throughout American history. The Affirmative Action Cookie Sale taught me a great lesson in life. Every time a fringe political movement arises that demands justice but does not fight for all Americans, I always find myself wondering: *Who is really paying for that cookie dough?*

The Old Man and the Parking Lot

Al Pacino is considered an icon in the Latino community for portraying a Cuban in *Scarface* and a Puerto Rican in *Carlito's Way*. When I was growing up, *Scarface* posters always hung next to Raiders flags in every garage I stepped into. But truthfully, nobody could get away with that very dated *Scarface* accent today, not even the great Al Pacino himself. Cubans watch that film today and are like, "What da fuck, mang!" I was rehearsing at UCLA working on my Chicano accent for a play that Jose Luis was directing—trying my best not to sound like Tony Montana—when *she* walked into our class. A short, brown firecracker of a woman named Lupe Ontiveros. Lupe had starred as the maid in over one hundred TV, film, and theater roles, including the Jack Nicholson–Helen Hunt comedy *As Good as It Gets*. Lupe was an older Mexican American lady with a big laugh and an even bigger sense of purpose.

She was a past social worker who started in theater with Jose Luis, and who would portray strong Latina women on-screen, like Nacha in *El Norte*, Carmen in *Real Women Have Curves*, and Juanita in *Desperate Housewives*. But it was playing Yolanda in the movie *Selena* that most stuck with me. Lupe was not at all like the treacherous character who shot Jennifer Lopez in the biopic of the Tejana superstar. Lupe walked into our rehearsal room unannounced, greeted Jose Luis, who knew to quickly get out of her way onstage, and she proceeded to talk about LALIFF: the Los Angeles Latino International Film Festival. She thought that as a bunch of young Latinos aspiring to work in the entertainment industry, we should consider volunteering for the film festival since it was the one place in town where the Hollywood industry and Latino community came together. We were all rehearsing for a Chicano theater festival. LALIFF sounded right up my alley. I decided to do what Lupe said. I mean, the woman did kill Selena!

LALIFF was an initiative launched by the City of Los Angeles when a passionate and highly dedicated woman named Marlene Dermer and the late Cuban film programmer George Hernandez on one end, and Latino Hollywood icon Edward James Olmos and his nonprofit partner Kirk Whisler on the other end, turned in competing bids for creating Los Angeles' first Latino International Film Festival. The city loved both bids so much that they asked the two factions to join forces, which was how LALIFF came to be. When I joined the Latino film festival as a volunteer, Marlene was basically a one-woman show, given that George Hernandez had sadly passed away, Kirk Whisler had moved on to run other nonprofits, and Edward James Olmos was filming his mega-hit TV series, *Battlestar Galactica*. Marlene was of Peruvian descent, so you know she and I were destined to go to war with each other over our deeply held beliefs of where ceviche came from. (Answer: Ecuador!) Marlene was a young single mother in life; thus, she was a resilient woman accustomed to working without the help of others. I saw so much of what my mom had to overcome in her early life in Marlene's story. I was eager to help.

I volunteered at LALIFF as much as I could after classes, but when the summer hit, I went all in. I volunteered to set up folding chairs for the youth program, to make purchase runs for the production department, to pick up lunch for the volunteers, to do anything that needed to be done. I was on the floor fixing the bottom of a desk one evening when *he* walked in: Emmy and Golden Globe–winning actor and activist Edward James Olmos. Olmos was best known for being the only Mexican American ever to be nominated for an Academy Award for Best Actor for his portrayal of East LA public school teacher Jaime Escalante in the film *Stand and Deliver*. I had hoped to one day meet Olmos, but in a different capacity—perhaps while I was at least standing up (pun intended). Olmos stopped at the table I was fixing, looked down at me, and said: "Thank you for all the work you're doing." It was quite ironic that the most successful actor from the Latino community at the time found me—literally—working under the table.

Here is an unsolicited tip to anybody wondering why

Edward James Olmos is such a legendary actor, or how they, too, can one day get to his level. Olmos always controlled the characters he portrayed. It's that simple. In *Blade Runner*, Ridley Scott did not ask him to invent a new futuristic Los Angeles language; he just did. In the original *Miami Vice*, he agreed to do Michael Mann's TV series only if he had complete creative control of Lieutenant Castillo, which meant he never had to do what the stars of the show demanded of him. In the groundbreaking musical *Zoot Suit*, while everyone was doing *teatro*, Olmos was performing Kabuki theater as El Pachuco. If you want to be a great artist, then you have to take full control of your art. Olmos did exactly that.

I was in the production office late one night when I found out that the LALIFF Opening Night Gala tickets were open for purchase to the public. Up until that point, I figured the big event was invite-only. I had seen invites go out to the likes of Andy Garcia and Rita Moreno; I never imagined commoners like myself could attend by simply paying. The gala tickets were expensive at almost one hundred dollars each, but I had been working so hard and I barely saw my parents. I thought this was a great way for them and my uncles to see what I had been spending my entire summer doing. I told my supervisor that I wanted to buy six gala tickets. Now that I was a permanent resident in this country, I could have luxury items such as a debit card. I didn't have much money in the bank. I had exactly six hundred dollars, which I used for the six LALIFF Opening Night Gala tickets for my family.

The big opening night arrived and I was ecstatic. I couldn't wait to see how an international film festival unfolded. But more important, I couldn't wait to see my parents and my uncles, who rarely allowed themselves an extravagance such as going to the movies, let alone going to a Hollywood opening night at the historic Grauman's Egyptian Theatre. Hell, I hadn't done that either! The giant searchlights on the street alerting the night sky that there was a major event in progress made the entire evening even more magical. I walked to the front entrance, past all the men in suits and women in gowns, and saw one of my colleagues sneak someone into the event. Then I saw another staff member do the same thing. I walked over to the box office and curiously asked if everyone in the team had bought their guests gala tickets. The box office coordinator looked at me with a concerned smile and said: "No. Just you."

I was shocked to discover that all the staff and volunteers were sneaking their friends and families into the gala. Funny enough, one of those people sneaking in was then-unknown, future megastar Eva Longoria. Today, Eva is a Hollywood iconoclast with open doors everywhere, and I'm still over here paying for my goddamn gala tickets!

I greeted my parents and my uncles and I guided them through the red carpet with our unnecessarily paid gala tickets. My mom and dad could not believe it. They were on an actual red carpet. *Dios mío.* They loved it, but quickly felt very out of place. They weren't made for the glitz and glamour of Hollywood. I showed them the historical courtyard, guided them through the renovated lobby, and showed them to their seats. I felt like I was still interpreting everything for my parents. Except this wasn't English; it was Hollywood. My parents and my aunts and uncles had a blast. How could they not? The evening cost me my life savings!

Post the Opening Night Gala, Marlene asked to speak to me. She said she'd heard I'd bought all six of my gala tickets: "Is that true?" Still bothered, I assured her that it was. Marlene was impressed. "I don't think anyone on the staff has ever done that before," Marlene said, now taking me in as much more than a volunteer. From that moment, Marlene never questioned my loyalty to the organization.

I was eating with the volunteers one day when Lupe Ontiveros showed up at the festival. Without any of us knowing, Lupe had personally called all the Mexican restaurants on Cesar E. Chavez Avenue that had donated the food for the LALIFF volunteers. Lupe was so giving of her time that she sat down with us and started cracking jokes. I didn't know if I would ever have the chance to speak to Lupe again, so I took it upon myself to ask: "Do you hate that you had to play so many maids in your career?" All the other volunteers went silent. While it wasn't my intention, the question was in poor taste. Lupe's response still sits with me to this day: "I played those roles so that nobody else would have to." *Wow.*

To beat the LA traffic from West Covina, I would arrive early at the festival. That was why the production department put me in charge of working with the people who ran the parking lot. We always needed to rent more parking spots for extra space, and that all had to be negotiated early in the morning. Most of the parking attendants were Latinos and they were always willing to help me out. Only one attendant was not. His name was John. He was a poor-looking parking attendant who was in his late eighties. I have no idea how he was even hired. But John's saving grace was that he was funny. He loved to crack jokes as he handed out his parking tickets. Every morning I would see John with clothes that didn't seem to fit him, always wearing a large, weathered straw hat to protect him from the unrelenting Southern California sun, and when the volunteer food would arrive, I would make him a plate. John wasn't a LALIFF volunteer so he wasn't entitled to our food, but I saw him every morning by himself handing out tickets in the blistering sun, and I felt bad for the guy. I figured he needed company and some good Mexican food.

A few days later, Marlene came running out of the theater freaking out. Someone had interrupted the screening she was presenting to inform her that we had lost a venue for a big party. Needless to say, somebody was about to lose their job. Trying to be helpful, I suggested the posh nightclub across the street called Les Deux. Marlene said that if I thought I could get the *it* club in town, then I should. I immediately walked over to speak to the Les Deux manager, who informed me that he was in the middle of a dispute with the owner of the building and doubted either of us could use the space that weekend. "Who is the owner?" I wondered. The manager told me that the owner of the building was the same owner of all the parking structures around town: "He's a very difficult man to get ahold of. Good luck."

I walked over to the main parking office. By this point, all the office staff knew me from the festival. I asked to speak to the owner. "Sure thing," said the Latina receptionist. When she escorted me to the executive office, I was blown away to see John sitting behind a big fancy desk. His old, weathered straw hat was just an arm's reach away.

"Rafael! What're you doing here?"

"John...you own the parking lot?"

"Of course."

"And you own Les Deux?"

John rolled his eyes and said, "Don't even get me started with that club."

"Umm...well...we wanted to rent it for the film festival."

"Anything for you, Rafael. You don't even gotta ask."

And that, ladies and gentlemen, was my first experience as a Hollywood producer.

Marlene very kindly told Mr. Olmos that I helped saved the festival that year. All the staff and volunteers wanted to know how I had pulled off getting the hottest club in Hollywood—and practically for free. The answer was easy, and it was also my greatest lesson in production: always be kind to everybody. Who would have known that the old parking attendant, who literally looked like a homeless man, and his family owned most of the real estate in Hollywood since the studios first started doing black-and-white film premieres at the Chinese Theatre. John was retired, reaching the end of his life, and when he wasn't volunteering with Army veterans, he was at the parking lot behind the Egyptian Theatre personally selling parking tickets to out-of-towners, telling very bad dad jokes. It just so happened that he took a liking to a wide-eyed immigrant kid volunteering for a Latino film festival that took place in the heart of Hollywood.

The Deported

At the film festival, I met a Spaniard named Gorka. This retired rock star was a riot. Not just because he was better looking than the movie stars he would assist on the red carpets as PR, but because he had an equal passion for spirituality and moderation as he had for extremities and living life to the fullest. Gorka would work all day with me as a volunteer, disappear for three hours, and then come back for a night shift. When I asked where he had been, Gorka would just shrug: "The Playboy Mansion."

There was another Spaniard, also from the Basque country, who ran press for the film festival. Her name was Miren, and she was a joyous woman who couldn't believe that people didn't smoke more cigarettes in California. Miren was a consummate professional and her work was outstanding. If she ever lost her cool, it was because you weren't doing your job.

Miren, Gorka, and I spent the entire two weeks of the festival hanging out. We became fast friends. I dropped them off at the airport and really hated saying good-bye to them. They invited me to visit them in Spain. Now that I had papers, I was seriously considering it. The only problem was that after spending my life savings on stupid gala tickets, I was broke.

After the film festival, Liesel and Steve called me unexpectedly. They always kept in close touch with me, and knew that I was disappointed I couldn't go visit my new friends in Spain. That was when they gave me the surprise of my life.

"We always felt bad that you couldn't go to Prague with the forensics team," explained Liesel.

"It also sucks that you were never able to travel outside of the country," added Steve.

"So we saved up enough frequent flyer miles for you to go to Spain and visit your friends," Liesel finally blurted out.

I was speechless. Ironic, given all our speech history together. After all the crushing debt and free volunteer work, Liesel and Steve were giving me a free trip to Europe. I was an emotional mess. But more important, I was going to mothaf*ckin' Spain!

———

As you may recall, I arrived in Madrid and was detained by immigration authorities for not having a special visa to enter Spain as an Ecuadorian citizen. That is why I was placed in a jail inside the airport awaiting deportation.

Flabbergasted, I asked the immigration official on the other side of the metal bars if I could please make a phone call.

He explained there was a public phone behind me, and that he sells calling cards at noon and at 6:00 p.m. every day. Since it was now noon, he could sell me one.

"Yes, please," I begged.

I exchanged what little money I had in my pocket for a calling card and rushed over to the pay phone, only to discover that there was a line of people waiting to use it. No matter how tough a gangbanger I'd pretended to be in middle school, I had never been inside a jail before. Sadly, the scene was exactly as they depicted on American television: a lot of desperate men waiting for their turn to call or eagerly anticipating for someone to call them. There was one other thing that was exactly like all the American prison shows I had seen up to that point: everybody in this European jail was Black. They all spoke Spanish, but they were all clearly of African descent. There were Afro-Cubans, Afro-Venezuelans, Afro-Colombians, and Afro-Panamanians. Like me, they were mostly from Latin America. Unlike me, they were all of darker pigmentation. This hit me like a ton of bricks. I had hoped that racism was an American invention like my light-skinned, privileged family in Ecuador always asserted. But here in front of my very eyes was proof that it didn't matter where you lived in the world; being Black was a detriment to your peaceful existence.

It was finally my turn to use the pay phone and I called Miren, who in turn was worried sick. She said she had waited outside the airport but I never came out. I explained my situation.

"You needed a special visa? *Joder!*"

Miren said she would call a friend of hers at the Spanish Consulate in Los Angeles to resolve this problem of the special visa, but that I should call the airline to get a refund for my flight. Miren was always so cool under pressure. I hung up with her and dialed Continental Airlines. I told the customer service representative of my plight, and she felt horrible for me. She said she would get me a brand-new—

"Hello? Hello!"

The line went dead. My calling card had run out of money, and just as I was about to get my entire flight refunded. Shit! I ran over to the jail bars and begged the immigration official for another calling card. The official casually looked up at the clock on the wall. It was now 12:20 p.m.

"As I mentioned, I only sell calling cards at noon and at six p.m.," he said calmly before going back to his newspaper.

At first I thought he was joking. But after he ignored my next two pleas for a calling card, I realized he was dead serious. He was not going to sell me a calling card. Defeated, I walked back to the bench by the pay phone and sat down. I was nervous. I didn't know what would happen to me.

There were a lot of nature posters, like tropical birds and serene waterfalls, hung up around the jail. The posters were from all over Latin America. They were clearly there to make the temporary residents of the jail feel more at home. I'm sad to report that there was a poster from Ecuador, and that it did, in fact, make me feel more at home. It's sad that I had to go all the way to Spain and get deported before I could start missing Ecuador. It was a poster of a tropical parrot in the Galápagos

Islands—a place most poor Ecuadorians could never afford to visit. It was now 5:50 p.m. and I had been in captivity for over seven hours. I was losing my mind. I walked over to the steel bars and asked the immigration official if he would now please sell me a calling card. Instead of looking at me, he casually glanced up at the wall, and since it was still a few minutes before 6 p.m., he went back to the paperwork on his desk. Just like in the movies, I hung on to the bars like a criminal with no possibility for parole. It must have been a very sad sight. When the clock finally hit 6:00 p.m., the official looked over at me and said something that made my blood boil. This motherf*cker said...

"How can I help you?"

I ran over to the pay phone with what I thought was enough calling cards to last me a lifetime. I started making all kinds of calls. I reconnected with Miren, who by this point had already created a step-by-step game plan of what I had to do when I got back to Los Angeles to get my special visa from the Spanish Consulate. I then connected with Gorka, who was able to secure a new train ticket for me so that I could get to Pamplona to see him. Then I called Continental Airlines. This time, however, I could not reconnect with the lovely female customer service agent who was so incredibly understanding. Instead, I connected to a miserable male representative, who wanted nothing to do with me. I told him about my unbelievable travel experience, but he wasn't having it.

"We were already fined five thousand dollars for letting you fly without the special visa," he said with a tone that you reserved only for unwanted children. "We don't owe you any-thing." In fear that my calling card would run out, I quickly switched my strategy to kindness and explained that I had already spoken to a female customer service representative, and she was going to get me a brand-new—

"Hello? Hello!"

The line went dead. My calling cards had all run out of money once more. This time, I didn't bother going back to the immigration official to get more.

I slept with my shoes on that night. I didn't like the way one of the immigrants in the jail was looking at my sneakers, so I didn't take them off. I also couldn't sleep because the guy on the metal bunk bed above me wouldn't stop crying. Accord-ing to him, getting into Spain was his only hope for providing for his family. I don't remember where the other people in our four-person cell came from, except the Russian. The Russian had a heartbreaking story. He had left his never-before-heard-of small town in Russia days before a deadly mass shooting there took over the international headlines. It was a horrific story that does not deserve to be repeated, but included a lot of small children. Because that never-before-heard-of small town was now all over the news, he was denied entrance into Spain. Like all the other immigrants, he had friends and family wait-ing for him with job opportunities ready to go. All were being denied these opportunities for being born in the wrong place or for being born with the wrong skin color.

The next morning, when it was time for me to be deported back to the United States, immigration enforcement was not subtle about any of it. They put me in handcuffs and mounted me on a small electrical cart that drove me up the stairs to the plane. Spanish police walked me to my seat, removed my handcuffs, and walked away as the unknowing passengers and flight attendants looked at me with terror. I'm sure they all thought I was a criminal at best, and a terrorist at worst. A good-looking terrorist, but a terrorist nevertheless. I arrived back in the United States, but I couldn't bring myself to go home. I didn't want to tell my parents what had happened. During my entire ordeal in Spain, I'd never once called my parents. I didn't want to burden them with my stupidity. I went to stay with Liesel and Steve, who felt horrible about the whole special visa situation. They felt that if they hadn't bought the ticket for me, this would have come up before I even stepped foot on the plane. But the world's arbitrary immigration laws were not their fault. Just like it wasn't their fault that we now lived within barricaded borders but existed in a borderless economy. I got my special visa expedited in a day from the Spanish Consulate in Los Angeles, thanks to Miren, and boarded a new flight to Spain that same day. I was able to get a new free flight thanks to Liesel. The airline customer service wouldn't listen to a broke Latino college student, but they sure as hell jumped when a customer that did a lot of business with them called to complain. Now at the airport ready to head back to Spain, I finally decided to call my parents. Excited to hear from me, they asked me where I was.

"Are you in Madrid with Miren?"

"No," I said.

"Oh—are you in Pamplona with Gorka?"

"Not yet."

"Are you in San Sebastian?"

"I'm with Steve and Liesel in LA. I was deported from Spain. But don't worry, I'm heading back now."

My parents were speechless.

It all sounded crazy coming out of my mouth. I can't even begin to imagine what my parents must have thought. I flew back across the Atlantic. I landed in Spain once again. When I exited the plane, I walked up to the same customs kiosk, and the same Spanish officer asked me for my immigration papers. He saw my Ecuadorian passport and quickly looked up at me—shocked to see that I was back for more. This time I dropped the special visa they required on top of my Ecuadorian passport, followed by my permanent residency card from the United States of America. I smiled. The Spanish officer begrudgingly stamped my Ecuadorian passport, which finally granted me access into Europe. I put my sunglasses back on and walked out of the Spanish airport triumphant. I looked around Madrid for the first time. It was beautiful. But I must admit, my heart ached when I saw nothing but predominantly white tourists entering the country.

The Comedy with the Name Nobody Wants to Say

Allan and Miles were close friends of mine from Mt. SAC. The three of us traveled a lot doing forensics together. But we didn't just do speech and debate: we destroyed the entire Western United States speech and debate scene. If I sound cocky, it's because we were two-year students taking on and beating the crap out of four-year students. We won speech tournaments at the local level, at the state level, and at the national level. And we did it while representing the three biggest minority groups in the country: Allan was Asian American; Miles was African American; and well, you know my story.

Allan and Miles both transferred to UCLA a year after I did. As I continued to commute to Westwood from my parents' house, Miles moved into the dorms while Allan found a cost-effective apartment to live in. Now that we were all at university together, the three of us hung out all the time. We looked like a walking United Colors of Benetton ad. It was an unwritten rule among us that one of them would usually have to take me in for the night if I was too tired to commute home. Eventually this evolved into Miles always sneaking me into the dorm cafeteria during the day, while Allan let me crash in his apartment at night.

It was around this time that I complained to Liesel and Steve about my experience at UCLA. Outside of Jose Luis and the one Chicano theater festival I was a part of, nothing spoke to me, and I still wasn't cast in anything on the main stage. I was starting to grow resentful from the lack of stories and roles for people of color in theater and began feeling like there would be no place for me in the entertainment industry as a whole that felt honest and real. Luckily, while still not enough representation, I discovered the theater work of John Leguizamo, Tim Miller, Anna Deavere Smith, and Spalding Gray. I wondered out loud if maybe I should write a one-man show.

"Oh, please don't," said an almost insulted Steve. "Those can be hard to watch sometimes."

"Why don't you get with Miles and Allan and put something together," suggested Liesel.

"Yeah, like a three-man one-man show," replied Steve, now a little more open to the idea.

Perhaps there was something to us uniting forces. Allan was getting into slam poetry at the time and Miles was just starting to work the stand-up circuit. I asked the guys if they were up to writing a new show with me. Sure, they thought, as long as they could fit it in between all their schoolwork.

The guys and I met up with Steve and Liesel, and it felt like old times. We had a shorthand with each other from those two solid years of doing forensics together. We quickly handed out assignments. Our first prompt: when was the first time you remember feeling different?

Allan and I took the assignment seriously. Of course, Allan was going to outshine all of us by talking about the first time he remembered hearing the word "chink" on the playground. He shared a heartbreaking story of learning from the girl he had a crush on that he wasn't as good-looking as Tom Cruise (the American heartthrob Allan idolized) because he was a "chink." My own writing was not as poignant, but it also had a lot to do with cultural identity because I talked about the year I dyed my hair blond and passed as white, and how cops stopped harassing me and girls started talking to me more. Miles, on the other hand, wrote a sketch about a Black Santa and how nobody would accept this nonwhite Santa at Christmas as he would most likely be forced to deliver toys to little children while doing community service. If Allan always found a way to exceed expectations in his assignments, Miles always knew how to blow them up and make them surprisingly hilarious.

I would work in the mornings at the UCLA law bookstore, then go to all my UCLA theater classes, before finally ending my evenings at Liesel and Steve's house putting together the building blocks of a new show. After reading Allan's story, we asked him what he did when the girl called him a "chink."

"Well," said Allan, "I told my mom and she said that maybe I could one day get the surgery."

"What's the surgery?" I asked naively.

The surgery was eyelid surgery, and it was quite common in Asian American communities. I was floored. I knew Allan, and his very sweet mother, so well, yet I had never heard of this specific incident in his life. I had no clue that mutilation of one's face was common in the global Asian community in an attempt to appear more Caucasian.

We then looked at my writing, which the group thought was okay, but none of them could understand why I was avoiding the most obvious difficulty I had to deal with: growing up undocumented in America. *Oh yeah*, I thought. There was that. I wasn't ready to talk about myself just yet, so I hid behind my parents' journey. I was receptive to the idea of sharing their story.

The Black Santa sketch Miles wrote was so incredibly funny that we were determined to use it in some capacity, but as everyone did with me, we tried to get Miles to dig a little deeper. We asked him if he remembered the first time he heard "the word." *Oh, did he!* Miles said it was in a predominantly white school, with his predominantly white friends as they read *Huckleberry Finn*. The word makes quite a few appearances in Mark Twain's novel. And while he had heard it before, it wasn't until the predominantly white class landed on it in the book and everyone turned to look at him that Miles ever related that word to himself. *Fuck*. That shit was heavy…but it was also a phenomenal story to share onstage! I was strangely jealous that Miles's racism story was better than mine.

As the show and its acts were taking shape, we still faced a major problem: what would the title be? We tried not to think about it too much, and just stayed focused on the writing. It was unbelievable to me that the three of us were so vastly different—and literally came from different parts of the world—yet shared that same commonalities of feeling othered at a very young age. These three derogatory terms that kept popping up during our writing process—nigger, wetback, chink—were all trying to place our unique cultural identities but we refused to let them.

With the play practically done, the five of us came together to brainstorm on a title. This was a safe space, and there were no bad ideas. We just started spitballing…

"The Race Show?"

"The Vocal Minority?"

"Ethnic Friends?"

"Race-ish?"

"America Redux?"

And then someone jokingly said: *"N*GGER WETB*CK CH*NK?"*

When a powerful title arrives, it truly lets itself be known. The problem, of course, was how controversial this title would be regardless of our intention of having a discussion around those hateful words. But they kept appearing in a lot of our writing. They were unavoidable. I must admit that *Ethnic Friends* was a close second, but none of us wanted to be sued for using the font of NBC's *Friends*. We chose the more difficult route: to have a dialogue about racist hate speech in America with the actual racist language.

We had our script and title, but now we needed money to put together our show. We needed costumes, sets, and a theater. It was my dream to be able to rent out the Freud Playhouse, which was reserved only for professional touring companies, like the Royal Shakespeare Company. *Goddamn it*, I thought. *Shakespeare strikes again.* I was determined to beat the Bard this time around. But alas, the Freud Playhouse was too expensive and out of our marginalized reach. That's when we came up with the idea to become a student group on campus. Student groups were eligible to apply for campus activities money. Campus activities money came out of our student fees, so we were just applying for the money we had already paid to the university as students. We discovered you only needed four things to become a student group at UCLA. One, have three members: Allan, Miles, and me. Two, have official titles: we all trusted Allan being our treasurer, but I beat Miles to the presidency by highlighting all the things my administration had accomplished while I was senior class president. Three, have a mission statement: we came up with something on the fly. And four, have a name. To this day, if you check the records of UCLA, you will discover there was a student group called N*GGER WETB*CK CH*NK, and that group applied for and received fifteen thousand dollars for our first production. By the way, we only got that funding because nobody in student government wanted to go on the record saying any of those words out loud, which you had to do to bring up any objections with any particular program being funded.

We quickly rented a theater on campus, set the date for our premiere, and then started marketing the show. The marketing was a great lesson on the difference between in-group and out-group jokes. If we had put up posters with our faces on it with our title, people might have gotten it. Instead we put up posters that simply stated "N*GGER WETB*CK CH*NK TONIGHT." Like Michelle Rodriguez, the uproar was fast and furious. We thought we might shock some people, but never at this magnitude. Ironically enough, the people who were most offended were not of African American, Latin American, or Asian American descent. Our posters were destroyed. Some people would rip off "N*GGER" but leave "WETB*CK" and "CH*NK" because those were okay. Others would cross out all three and write "honky honky honky." Some people just took the signs home with them. We were an official student group, so we had full permission to advertise the show on campus. I was forced to file a police report on our stolen posters, and when I told the seasoned white police officer the title of our show, he looked me directly in the eyes and all he said was: "How do you spell 'chink'?"

The night of our first performance, we were nervous wrecks. None of us had invited our parents. We were just focusing on not forgetting our lines and hoping that enough people showed up to justify our renting the 300-seat auditorium. I had never spent that much money on anything before. It didn't help that a small group of protesters came to picket our show. For one hot second, we did think we'd made a huge mistake putting this show together. But then, out of nowhere, the audience came out in droves. The auditorium could only seat 300 people, but 450 people showed up. There was so much excitement around the show that the protesters gave up and joined the line to try to get in themselves. We got in trouble with the venue because people broke the exit door to sneak in and watch the show. It was mayhem. And then we took the stage.

I still cry thinking about those early performances. There was so much riding on a single show. On one level, we wanted people to like our writing. On another level, we wanted people to like our acting. And on yet another, we wanted people to like us as human beings. The response and the reaction to that first night were overwhelming. Buzz quickly built around campus. Who were these guys? What was this show? And what hunger did they tap into that everyone seemed to suddenly want to talk about race? Then we did what no other student group had ever done before: we walked up to the Freud Playhouse and handed them a check from the earnings we'd made in the first two shows. We rented out the professional touring theater. We were now set to take the main stage at UCLA.

Hugh Hart, an *L.A. Times* journalist, heard about our show and wanted to come witness it for himself at the Freud Playhouse. Unfortunately, the night of the Freud performance it started to rain. Being that it was Los Angeles, we feared that nobody would show up, and that the nearly six-hundred-seat Freud Playhouse would be empty except for Hugh himself. But that wasn't the story that was meant to be. Instead, the *L.A. Times* journalist wrote about how hundreds of people stood in the cold and in the pouring rain, wrapped around the theater, just to experience a show that had now developed a cult following. He titled the piece: "Nasty Words, Wicked Fun." Hugh's article created even more buzz for us.

My theater mentor, Jose Luis, pulled me aside after our two sold-out Freud Playhouse performances and in a stoic fashion said, "I cannot say the title of your play, but it's important and I want to produce it at the Los Angeles Theater Center." And just like that, *NWC* was prepped for its first union, professional run in downtown LA. Packing the show with hundreds of college students was one thing. A general audience of judgmental Angelenos who only went to theater in LA if it was produced by Center Theatre Group was quite another.

Now with the support of the Latino Theater Company, we continued the success of *NWC* in Los Angeles. Liesel and Steve stepped up to codirect the show. Additionally, Steve oversaw the new set and costume designs, while Liesel focused on tech and lighting design—leaving Miles, Allan, and me free to work on our performances and postshow Q&As, which we knew there would be a ton of. We quickly built an audience in downtown LA, and it began selling out. I partially credit our success to my family. You know I had so many friends and aunts and cousins that we sold out the first two weeks without

a problem. The Latino Theater Company also had a remarkable following, so the affluent Latinos came out in droves. We
extended the run in downtown twice, and the only reason we
had to put an end to it was not because there was a lack of
interest, but because we had finals. Allan and I were the first
in our families to graduate from college in the United States.
For that reason, kicking ass on our finals was more important
than the dream of having an extended sold-out theater run in
Los Angeles. *NWC*, however, achieved both.

After the three of us graduated from UCLA (Allan and
Miles with their BAs and me with my MA), the five of us col-
lectively signed with a management company. But not just
any management company. David Lieberman was a master
of touring performing arts centers. He managed the who's
who of national touring companies. He represented The
Actors' Gang, Merce Cunningham Dance Company, Circle
in the Square, the Watts Prophets, Kronos Quartet, and now
N*GGER WETB*CK CH*NK. In case you were doing the
math in your head, we went from a student show to a professional run in downtown LA to a national tour in just three
months.

Guy in Kentucky

We toured the nation for three straight years. The *L.A. Times* compared *NWC* to the comedy of Chris Rock and early Culture Clash, while the *Seattle Intelligencer* declared we were "the anti-Three Stooges—nobody's fools, and nobody's victims." Everywhere we went, people were up in arms about the title but then responded incredibly well to the show itself. We, however, were exhausted. We were on the road nine months out of the year. The stresses of a national tour and co-owning a business were getting to us. Liesel and Steve knew how to launch successful companies, but Miles, Allan, and I were learning those hardships for the first time. To use a phrase that Allan educated me on: I began to see the chink in the armor. We worked so hard at putting on a great show for people, while trying our best to pay our bills and balance our books, that we forgot to work on our friendship.

Liesel took a sabbatical from college to tour with us that first year, but by year two she had to go back to Mt. SAC, and

Allan, Miles, Steve, and I continued on the road without her. Liesel still handled most of our touring logistics from home for us, while Steve became mother hen on the road and the "token white guy" holding the mic for us during Q&As. By the way, Steve had just cocreated the animated hit series *Ben 10* for Cartoon Network and *still* he insisted on being on the road to help us out! But by the end of the second year of touring, we stopped going out together after the shows. As the tour became grueling to us, we started to stay in our separate hotel rooms more. Believe it or not, the power of *NWC* was not the performance; it wasn't even the comedy. It was the audience. We weren't always changing lives, but *NWC* forced people to look inward as they laughed. The title was always controversial and part of our discussion at all times. Fortunately, a big part of the project was to have residencies in every community we visited in order to have dialogues and workshops about issues in the show. This very meaningful work, however, took a toll on all of us. I'm sure some of the audience members were laughing without any deeper introspection, but as long as one person got it, that made all the touring worthwhile. If you don't believe me, just listen to what happened in Kentucky.

We performed the entire show and then held a Q&A afterward. We secretly disliked doing these Q&As because we felt the audience needed time to digest the show before they could start asking us questions. But it was really the Q&As and the community dialogue that our management company was selling, so we had to do them. A young, skinny bespectacled white guy in the front row raised his hand to ask a question. As Steve hurried over to him with the mic, we realized that he was crying. Miles, Allan, and I looked at each other and thought, *This is a comedy, what did we do wrong?* The guy with glasses, now holding the microphone, didn't have a question. He simply wanted to say:

"I've only cried twice in my life. The first time was during *Titanic*."

Wow. What a brave soul to admit that out loud.

"And second," he continued, "was during this show. Because as you told your stories, I related to you. And I realized that I had never related to a minority before because the only minorities I had ever seen were getting arrested on TV. I just wanted to say thank you—and that I promise to work on that."

Despite our building tension, the guys and I felt it was important to keep the show going. That comment made us feel like *Schindler's List*: "He who saves one life saves the world entire." I'm not trying to compare *NWC* to Jewish law, but the show did give us purpose. Whenever we grew tired of performing, all we had to do was remember that skinny white kid in Kentucky.

We arrived in Olympia, Washington, shortly after our Kentucky performance. Unfortunately, it was on the same weekend the NAACP was having a burial for the N-word. Bad timing all around. The local NAACP chapter no longer wanted people to say the word, and in a symbolic act were holding a literal burial for it. This was not good for us because we had to say the word in order to do the show. If that wasn't bad enough, the Sheriff's Department came backstage as we were getting ready to perform and informed us that they had intercepted some Neo-Nazi activity online. Olympia, Washington, was once a hotbed for the KKK, and Neo-Nazis were active and upset about our show coming to town. Apparently, Neo-Nazis thought *N*GGER WETB*CK CH*NK* was a show designed to bash white people. I'm guessing Neo-Nazis don't like to read because they didn't seem to read our title. Where does it mention white people? The Sheriff's Department took the time to walk us through what to do in case there was a race riot inside the theater. Before we took the stage, we heard members of the NAACP protesting our show outside. Then, a few Neo-Nazis also showed up to protest our show. There was never a race riot inside the theater in Olympia, Washington, but Black people and white people stood outside the theater united in their hatred of our show. I am by no means equating a hate group to a group that is actually fighting for the betterment of marginalized communities. All I'm pointing out is that *NWC* brought people together unlike you would ever imagine.

Like all great bands, *NWC* would eventually break up. Not from any lack of interest, but because the three of us were too young and needed time to reflect on what it was that we wanted out of life. I knew what I wanted. *NWC* was it. I got to write and star in something I'd created. There was so much power in that. But ultimately, *NWC* was like a marriage that needed to be worked on every day, and we didn't. It was too much recognition, too fast. I wish we had created it a little later in our lives, but—no matter what—we will always have that guy in Kentucky.

Tom Bradley International

On one of my stops back home from touring, my dad pulled me aside and asked me, "How would you feel if your mother and I moved back to Ecuador?" I appreciated that he asked but I was honestly more curious to know how he felt about it. He said he had been watching me pursue my dreams, and wanted to do the same. He wanted to be a surgeon again. My dad knew it would be hard to convince my mom to leave me, but he was aware that, at almost fifty, he had only so many years left of "his hands" (it's a surgeon thing). He had only one more shot to see if he still had it. But he wanted to know how I would *feel*?

"I think you should do it," I said, feeling like he'd sacrificed so much for me and my own dreams. I felt like it was his turn to pursue his, even if it hurt me to see them go.

The most heart-wrenching pain I've ever felt was saying good-bye to my mom. We were at LAX once again, but this time she was hopping on a plane with a one-way ticket to Ecuador. I didn't want her to leave. But while I was off touring, my parents had decided that I was old enough and successful enough to take care of myself. Without me knowing, my mom had prevented my dad from returning us to Ecuador when I was in high school. She thought I was too young to leave behind or disrupt my education. But when he broached the subject again post college, my mom no longer had any excuses. I admired my parents for wanting to return to Ecuador to be doctors again, but that didn't mean I was ready to put an entire continent between my mom and me.

The two of us were alone at the airport because my dad had left a few weeks earlier to look for a house in Guayaquil. When he left, I thought he would be back. But he never came back. He was eager to set roots in Ecuador. I get it. Can you imagine going fifteen years without seeing the people you love? My dad played his cards perfectly. He was starting to get paranoid about the housing market. They became homeowners immediately after getting their permanent residencies, but real estate value wouldn't stop rising. My dad thought it was too good to be true. No country could sustain this kind of housing market, not even the great United States of America. My dad was certain it was all going to collapse. He was new to the real estate game, but all of this seemed too fishy. That's when he realized that if he was ever going to try to go back to Ecuador to be a doctor again, now was the time. He had one shot to cash out before it was too late. The year was 2007. The housing market crashed one year after my parents left.

Tom Bradley International

My mom and I hugged each other tight inside the Tom Bradley International Terminal. I never knew why people hated airports so much until the very moment I had to say good-bye to my mom. I watched her go through security and walk toward her gate. Every step she took away from me was more painful than the last. We had gone through so much together in this country. As I watched her get farther and farther into her gate, I chose to believe that my mom was off searching for her own piece of the American Dream, just in a different part of America—*South* America.

The decision to return to Ecuador was possible only because of our permanent residencies. My parents would never have dared to leave if they had still been undocumented; otherwise they would not have been allowed back into the country. Our new legality allowed my mom and dad to imagine something different for themselves. They would have rather lived in the United States doing what they were put on this earth to do: saving children's lives. But since they couldn't make their dreams work here, they packed up and headed out in search of a better life... just like they did fifteen years earlier. Only this time, I wasn't by their side.

George Washington's Right-Hand Man

A year after my parents left, I received a letter from Homeland Security stating that I could now begin the application process to become a United States citizen. I had to take a moment to process what I was holding in my hands. I truly never thought this moment would come. And it was bittersweet because I was about to go through the entire process alone.

The most important part of the citizenship application process is the American history test. This was one exam I was not about to fail. I began to cram overtime. I read as many history books as I could, which only added to the vast knowledge of America I got from those old *Encyclopedia Britannicas* I still owned. I had taken those old encyclopedias with me from one new place to another. It was very masochistic of me.

Soon after submitting my application, I found myself in yet another federal building in downtown Los Angeles. The day had arrived. I was summoned to take my verbal citizenship test. I wasn't as nervous as I thought I would be. There was no way this federal examiner was going to stump me. Not on the day I had been waiting for since I learned I was undocumented.

The government official administering the test was a kind-looking Filipino American. But since there were a lot of people waiting to see him, there wasn't much time for pleasantries. He got right down to business. Following his lead, I answered his questions as quickly as he asked them of me...

"What is the supreme law of the land?"

"The constitution."

"How many original colonies were there?"

"Thirteen."

"How many amendments are there in the constitution?"

"Twenty-seven."

The speed at which I responded seemed to annoy him. I made a wrong calculation about what he was after. I think perhaps he wanted me to take my time. I was now getting a bit nervous. I did not want to mess up my only opportunity at becoming American.

The government official sat up straight in his chair and started glancing through his document, looking for harder questions to ask. But I did not back down.

"Who is the chief justice of the United States?"

"John Roberts."

"How many years do we elect senators for?"

"Six."

"What are two cabinet-level positions?"

"Secretary of State and Secretary of Defense."

The federal worker put down his papers and then reached into a drawer in his desk. Believe it or not, he brought out another set of questions. At this point, I started to freak out. But again, I did not relent.

"What line divides the North and the South?"

"The Mason-Dixon Line."

"Who was George Washington's right-hand man as he crossed the Delaware?"

Wait, what?

Oh fuck. I didn't know this one. Who was George Washington's right-hand man as he crossed the Delaware? Who the hell was George Washington's right-hand man as he crossed the Delaware! I didn't know. I could see the stupid painting right in front of me. I could see George Washington looking straight ahead, determined on his small ferry boat, getting his Captain Morgan on. The federal worker stared at me—was he hoping I would give up? I refused. I had come too far and endured way too much. There had to be an answer. There's always an answer. Who else is in this painting? Damn it—*who?* I could even see the ice being pushed away from the boat. Why couldn't I see George Washington's right-hand man?

"Well?" asked the federal worker.

After a long, painful pause, I finally surrendered. I said: "I'm sorry. I don't know."

To which the federal worker responded: "I don't know either, but if you knew that shit—holy hell!"

Shocked, I started to laugh from the nerves. The federal worker smiled, and then added: "Congratulations. You passed with flying colors."

I called my mom via Skype to tell her the great news. She was incredibly happy for me. It was strange not to be able to hug her at that moment, but this was our new reality now. We were connected digitally via the Internet and nothing more. My mom said that my dad also sent his congratulations. He wasn't home. He was operating at the hospital. He was rarely home when I Skyped. I thought Ecuador would be easier for him. Instead, it ended up being harder. He said it was the price he had to pay to do what he loved in a country that had a bad economy.

Four months later, I drove down the Interstate 10 to the Pomona Fairplex. I had been there a few times before for the LA County Fair. But this time was different. This occasion was special. I was being sworn in as an American citizen.

The ceremony felt like a bad TV game show. The Pomona hall was exceptionally large, packed with family members cheering on their loved ones. I, of course, showed up alone. Without my parents in the country, I just took the ceremony as another event in the middle of a very busy workweek. It was just another check mark off my calendar. The MC—there was an MC!—kept things lively and moving like a reality competition show on steroids. He asked us to guess what countries had the most people becoming citizens on that day.

"Coming in at number five," he said cheerfully, "Guatemala!"

The audience hooted and hollered.

"Number four...China!"

The audience clapped loudly.

"Number three...El Salvador!"

Louder cheers still.

"Number two....the Philippines!"

The place erupted.

Thinking there was no way it could possibly get any louder, the MC then said: "And coming in at number one...Mexico!!!"

After regaining my hearing from the volcanic eruption, we all eased into a video projected onto the large screen. It was of President George W. Bush welcoming us to the United States. This was perhaps the most bizarre thing of all, since it had just been revealed that we'd gone to war with Iraq for no apparent reason, and all of us present were being asked to swear we were of good moral character or lose the ability to become naturalized citizens.

As we were being lectured on American values by our sitting president, I glanced over at the gorgeous young woman sitting next to me. Earlier, she had told me she was from Bulgaria. She looked like someone you might see in a Victoria's Secret catalog. She also dressed like somebody you would see in a Victoria's Secret catalog, which didn't seem appropriate for a family-friendly ceremony. The young Bulgarian kept waving at her American husband, who stood nearby with all the onlookers behind the stanchions. He was an out-of-shape sixty-year-old man, who was ecstatic that his new young wife was finally becoming a citizen. I know that love is blind, but somebody was definitely using somebody in this scenario. I looked back at George W. Bush, a mediocre student in school who had not achieved half the things my undocumented friends had in college, and smiled at the irony.

I drove back home from the Pomona Fairplex that day as an American citizen. I thought about my parents and how if they had waited just two more years, the three of us could have all been sworn in together. But everyone's journey in life is different. My journey was that of a blissfully stupid American kid who discovered he wasn't American at all. It could have stopped me. It could have stopped us. But it didn't. We rallied together like all immigrant families do. We were just three people out of twelve million undocumented Americans—and sixty million Latinos—in this country who dared to dream of something better for themselves. We worked hard, we strengthened the economy, we made local food taste better, and we committed no crimes. Well, at least we committed the same crime as every other American family before us, or did we not want to take Native Americans into consideration for this story?

I drove down the Interstate 10 and remembered the moment I discovered I was undocumented. When I asked my mom why she never told me the truth of our immigration problems. Her response still astonishes me to this day...

"We didn't want you to grow up feeling different. Because dreams should not have borders."

No, Mom, they should not.

Epilogue

One of the earliest memories I have of being sick involve my mom and grandma. I don't remember what I was suffering from, but given that we lived in very hot Guayaquil, I'm sure it had something to do with some kind of tropical stomach virus. My mom, a young woman at the time still fighting her way through medical school, and my *abuelita*, a very traditional matriarch eager to pass down her longtime family healing remedies, were both ready to cure me.

My mom took my temperature, asked me to drink some warm water, and then gave me a pill to swallow that would make me feel better. Modern medicine fast at work. The story would have ended there, but my grandma then handed my mom a shiny small, round container. My mom smiled, and then took some of the concoction from inside it and gently spread it across my chest. For the life of me, I couldn't figure out what it was—or how its powers worked. All I knew was that I immediately started to feel better. The Ecuadorian concoction took hold of my body completely. Its healing abilities were clearly taking effect. I don't know why, but I started to feel more myself; I started to feel healed. The cool, homemade gel-like substance overtook my senses. For one perfect moment, my body was connected to the memories of my ancestors. More so than any medicine my mother could have given me, my grandma's homemade remedy was the stuff of legend. Lacking any real strength, I asked my grandma: "What is that?" With all her years of wisdom behind her, she calmly replied: "It's *vivaporu.*" She then added the magical Spanish rhyme that has healed all Latin American children throughout the centuries: "*Sana sana, colita de rana.*"

If you don't speak Spanish, you should know that *Sana sana, colita de rana* literally translates to: *Heal heal, frog ass.* But things tend to get lost in translation. For people who speak Spanish, *Sana sana, colita de rana* is gospel. It has always been with us, and it has always helped heal us.

Whenever I got sick in the United States, I always wished I had some of Grandma's *vivaporu.* What was in that sacred concoction? What was in that sacred word? I had never heard the word before my *abuelita* said it to me as I recovered that day: "*vivaporu.*" Maybe the word itself was Quechua. Quechua was the language spoken by the indigenous people of the Andes Mountains of South America. Quechua was also the official language of the Inca Empire. If you don't think the Incas could have created a medical ointment that could cure the sick, then you know nothing about the Inca Empire. For starters, it was the largest empire the New World had ever seen. Whereas the Aztecs were known as the warriors and the Mayans as the philosophers, the Incas were known as the empire builders. Their reach and influence were vast and wide. A central government, a unified language, aqueducts, cooking raw seafood with lime (i.e., ceviche), all of this was first present in the Americas because of the Incas. The country of Ecuador was part of the Inca Empire. In fact, one of the last Inca emperors, Huayna Cápac, loved Ecuador so much that he asked for his body to be buried in Peru (the Inca capital), but for his heart to be buried in Ecuador (the Inca spiritual center).

Vivaporu. Why did I receive it only as a child and never again as an adult? I always felt the reason I never received this Inca treatment past childhood was that we left Ecuador. I was being punished. This was my ancestors' way of showing their disapproval of me abandoning South America. It was also because of my *abuelita.* I rarely had her by my side once I left Ecuador. And my mom and dad—a medical couple—could never find a sickness that a simple injection could not fix. I could never stay home sick from school because I could never lie to them about being sick in the first place, or because one stupid injection had me cured within the hour.

After many years of being away, I returned to Ecuador for the first time in a long time to visit my parents. I was eager to visit my grandma's house. The house I was born in. It was exactly as I remembered it. Except that in my memories, the house was much larger. I felt like a giant walking through the hallways of my recollections. I walked into the old room my mom and I shared before we moved in with my dad, when she was still a single mother, and suddenly I remembered my mom and grandma nursing me back to health. Excited, I turned to my grandma and said, "Can you take me to go get some *vivaporu*?" My *abuelita* smiled; she could not wait to take me on this journey. It was finally time.

My grandma eagerly started to get ready. For her, any excuse to leave the house was a good excuse. She was happy to be spending time with me, as was I with her. But if I could be completely honest, I was most excited—almost nervous—to finally be able to get my hands on *vivaporu* once again. I didn't care how far we had to travel, or how much I had to spend. Today was going to be the day that I was reunited with our sacred medicine.

My grandma and I walked outside, but I was surprised to learn we weren't hailing a cab. She said we could get *vivaporu* just down the street. I always figured that my *abuelita* made the ointment by hand at home, but it also made perfect sense that she had a shaman-type friend in the neighborhood. I'd heard about what the *brujeria* women in town would do to their men for cheating on them. Perhaps they were also responsible for the *vivaporu*.

My grandma led me inside a convenience store. I figured that she needed to restock her calcium pills before we went to her friend's house. She walked down one of the small home-remedy aisles and waved me over. Curious, I approached and she handed me a small blue box. She was very pleased with herself. The small box contained an ointment bottle, which was the exact shape I remembered seeing in my memory as a sick little boy. I opened the box, pulled out the small round container, and read the label…

I almost dropped the bottle and shattered the magical ointment everywhere. In the movie version of my life, that's exactly what would've happened. It's that moment in the film when you figure out who Keyser Söze is; when you suddenly realize Borat was sent to America to spread the coronavirus unsuspectingly. My whole world stopped as I read the label and realized for the first time that *vivaporu* was really Vicks VapoRub.

That's right. Vicks mothaf*ckin' VapoRub! That was the indigenous healing ointment from my childhood. I had been longing for this corporate healing potion for nearly two decades, and it was the same Vicks VapoRub I had down the street from my house all along. I never hated my people's lack of enunciation more so than that very moment. It also dawned on me at this time that the Russian cologne "Mikhail Hordan," which my Ecuadorian cousin was proudly wearing, was really: Michael Jordan.

Discovering that *vivaporu* was Vicks VapoRub was the second most shocking revelation I ever made in my life. The first was discovering that my mom and my dad had gotten a divorce.

I saved this last tidbit until the end because it is still very painful to talk about. But even then, it was important that I didn't pass judgment on Enrique (my dad) as I wrote this book. I wanted to leave the wonderful memories of us together throughout my childhood untouched and unharmed. I leave those memories inside this book to be guarded by time. No one will ever take them away from me, not even Enrique himself.

As for my mom, she continues to inspire me with her resilience. She first showed me the courage and strength that it took to come to a new country, not knowing the language, the culture, or even having a career. Now she is showing me what it takes to return, pick up the broken pieces of your heart, and start anew. As remarkable as it sounds, my mom separated from her husband of thirty-four years, got COVID-19 two months into the start of the global pandemic, and was able to survive both.

My mom got on a plane once again and headed toward an uncertain future with only half a smile on her face but with a courageous open heart. The only silver lining was that this time around, she didn't journey away from me, but to me.

As I embraced my mom inside LAX, happily reunited with her after more than a decade apart, I found myself saying one simple phrase: *"Sana sana, colita de rana."*

Acknowledgments

This book was incredibly painful to write. It's not easy to look back at your life and discover some of the truths you held on to were lies all along. As always, I thank my beautiful family—both the biological and selected—for the great memories throughout the years. I look forward to creating many more together. And like my Tata used to say: *"Y el que diga que no . . . la p*#@ que lo parió!"*

There were several stories omitted from this memoir per the request of the people I lived them with. Also, the names of the young ladies I was romantically involved with were changed in an attempt to protect their identities. However, I do need to acknowledge Jane Becerra, who was willing to marry me after high school to help me with my immigration problems. The scared teenager I once was will forever thank you, Jane.

I want to personally thank Johanna Castillo, who initially tried to sign me when she was a book editor and then scooped me up when she became a book agent. There are not many

ACKNOWLEDGMENTS

Ecuadorian Americans who were on *People en Español*'s "most powerful women" list, so thank you for believing in me as an author before I even believed in myself.

Similarly, I need to thank my editor, Suzanne O'Neill. It's an awful lot of work to collaborate with a first-time author, so thank you for taking this book on after having worked on such phenomenal memoirs by the likes of Mindy Kaling and Jim Gaffigan. I'm proud to know that I'm somewhere at the bottom of your greatest hits!

Thank you to Ma and Pa Kent. America feels like a better place because of the love I—and a bunch of other college students—have received from Liesel Reinhart and Steven T. Seagle. As you two continue to expand your family, remember that I was your first adoptive son.

To my *NWC* family, which started with my brothers Miles Gregley and Allan Axibal, continued with Daisuke Tsuji, and came to a glorious conclusion with Jackson McQueen and Dionysio Basco. It means the world to me that we got to tour the United States together and change people's hearts one performance at a time.

To my boys: Sal Acosta, Napoleon Quezada, and Tommy Richardson. I love you guys with all my heart. West Cochina forever!

To my cousins—Ivan "Choli" Arrata, Raul Cruz, Priscilla Monserrate-Sanders, Diana Arrata, Jessica Monserrate, Juan Pablo Haz, Liz Arrata, and the philosopher-king Joseph Miller. Thank you for always treating me like your brother.

To the homies Steven Garcia, Kenny Zhou, and Ashley

Platz—we need to get back on a yacht ASAP! All kidding aside, Steven, thank you for the great book title. And, Ashley, thank you for saving my life...

To Mr. Moser and all the brave teachers at West Covina High School that had to put up with me. I'm sorry. As you can see, I was dealing with a lot at the time.

To the Mt. SAC forensics (speech and debate) team. Keep making us proud! And to my former AFA Duo Championship partner, Tasse Godinez. Rest in peace, my friend.

To my beautiful brown brothers and sisters from UCLA TFT, and to the man who held us all together, Jose Luis Valenzuela. Thank you.

To the Latino trailblazers in Hollywood who believed in me when nobody in the industry would. I would not have a career today if not for Gina Rodriguez, Wilmer Valderrama, Pete Corona, Flavio Morales, and the great Edward James Olmos.

To my Hollywood agent, Kyle Loftus. I'm still waiting for you to make me the Latino 50 Cent!

To the public school students of the Youth Cinema Project. I cannot wait to see the brilliant careers (in Hollywood or otherwise) you will all have. If I could go from being an English learner to writing an English-language memoir, then you can accomplish anything.

To the filmmakers and fellows of the Los Angeles Latino International Film Festival (LALIFF). I learn so much from you each and every day. You help redefine what it means to be American with your work.

ACKNOWLEDGMENTS

To the many people who have greatly impacted my life these past few years. There are too many of you to mention, but that's not going to stop me from trying: Pyet DeSpain, Bonny Garcia, Wendy Carrillo, Ali LeRoi, Alexis Tirado, Eloy Mendez, Ruben Garcia, Tonantzin Esparza, Erika Sabel Flores, Ray Jimenez, Marvin Lemus, Nicolas Barili, Alyssa Milano, Corinne Brinkerhoff, Kaitlin Saltzman, Patty Rodriguez, Gorka Urzaiz, Jose Antonio Vargas, Miren Gea, Bambadjan Bamba, Judy Baca, Scott Sanders, Mabel Arrambide, Julio Salgado, Ana-Christina Ramon, Curly Velasquez, Jeremy Berry, Eric Ro, Marlena Rodriguez, Tiffany Grant, Diana Cadavid, Adam Martinez, Alexis Garcia, Bodie Olmos, Magdiela Duhamel, Frank Williams, Pilar Flynn, Bryan Dimas, Uriel Saenz, Jennie Snyder Urman, Julio Anta, Erick Galindo, Danube Hermosillo, Wendy Rivadeneira, Paul Wilson, Mike Alfaro, Valentina Garza, Steven Zubkoff, Carolina Rivera, Jen Goyne Blake, Corina Calderon, Anibal Romero, Nzinga Blake, Jay Nomura, Mara Topic, Alexis de la Rocha, Carlos Salazar, Alicia Marie Agramonte, Rick Miller, Andrea Rivadeneira, Isabel Allende, Cristela Alonzo, Joaquin Castro...Okay, I lied. There are way too many of you. I'm sorry I cannot mention you all, but I do love you!

To my godchildren, Emilia Landivar and Salvador Acosta IV. Never stop learning. Please remember that human beings are like plants: if we're not growing, we're dying.

To Sergio "Chochis" Monserrate. You were born a day after me because you were destined to learn from my mistakes. You're a better leader, storyteller, and person than I'll ever be. It is the great privilege of my life that I get to be your older brother.

To Enrique... I truly hope you found the happiness you've been searching for your whole life. I keep the memories we shared close to my heart because they were real to me.

And to my mom, Violeta Lucia Arrata. Everything I've accomplished in my life is because of your love, your example, and your insistence on allowing me to dream freely, wildly, and without limitations.

About the Author

Rafael Agustin was a writer on the award-winning CW show *Jane the Virgin*. He is a Sundance Fellow for his TV family comedy *Illegal*, based on his life as a formerly undocumented American. Agustin cocreated and costarred in the national touring, award-winning autobiographical comedy *N*gger Wetb*ck Ch*nk*, which received acclaim from the *L.A. Times*, the *New York Times*, and the *Denver Post,* and won awards for its advancement of social justice in the arts. He serves as CEO of the Latino Film Institute (LFI), where he oversees the Youth Cinema Project, the Los Angeles Latino International Film Festival (LALIFF), and LatinX in Animation. In 2018, the *LA Weekly* named Agustin one of the fifty most essential people in Los Angeles. In 2021, Agustin was appointed to the National Film Preservation Board at the Library of Congress. Agustin received his BA and MA from UCLA's School of Theater, Film & Television and is an alumnus of the CBS Diversity Comedy Showcase.